D0410762

HIP**HOUSEPLANTS**

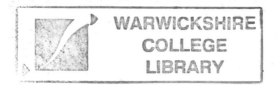
HIP**HOUSEPLANTS**

ORLANDO HAMILTON
PHOTOGRAPHY BY JEREMY HOPLEY

A Dorling Kindersley Book

Dorling **DK** Kindersley

LONDON, NEW YORK, SYDNEY, DELHI,
PARIS, MUNICH and JOHANNESBURG

Project Editor   **Neil Lockley**
Senior Art Editor   **Wendy Bartlet**
Category Publisher   **Judith More**
Art Director   **Janis Utton**
Horticultural Consultant   **Andrew Mikolajski**
Contributor   **Lynn Bryan**
Stylist   **Wei Tang**
Production Controller   **Louise Pope**
DTP Designer   **Sonia Charbonnier**

First published in Great Britain in 2001
by Dorling Kindersley Limited,
80 Strand, London WC2R ORL

2 4 6 8 10 9 7 5 3 1

Copyright © 2001
Dorling Kindersley Limited

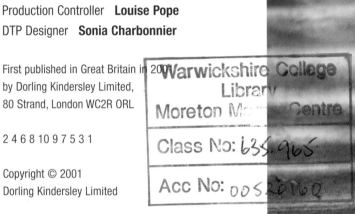

A CIP catalogue record for this book is available
from the British Library.

ISBN 0 7513 3382 4

Reproduced by Colourscan Overseas Co. Pte. Ltd.,
Singapore
Printed and bound by LEGO, Italy

see our complete catalogue at
www.dk.com

CONTENTS

FOREWORD

It may seem odd that I use the word "Hip" in conjunction with "houseplants" because to some readers they appear to be incompatible. However, I believe that houseplants are ready for a deserved comeback, and when chosen carefully can play a pivotal role in modern interior decorating schemes. This book aims to show how the right choice of plant and container will make an invaluable contribution to enhancing and defining your living space.

For me, the adventure with plants and flowers started at boarding school where I had my own allotment and grew my own fruit and vegetables. Several years later, while working in the City, I was invited by a lady called Jennifer d'Abo to join her very prestigious flowershop. After leaving school my initial interest in growing plants had waned, and I was probably as likely as the next person to buy my flowers outside a petrol station. Although it seemed like a complete volte-face, I accepted the offer and there started my new love affair with the horticultural world.

I am aware that the idea of cultivating plants indoors can be a daunting one, and I occasionally encounter people who regard themselves as serial houseplant killers. For them I have included plants that are low-maintenance and fall into what I call the "Terminator" category – difficult to kill. But there are also plants for the more adventurous that require love and attention.

Plants indoors are good for the soul (whether by their colour or scent). Plants can be soothing or they can lift the spirits, but their most valuable benefit is that they can deliver style. I hope that *Hip Houseplants* will show you why they are always worthy of their inclusion in our homes.

Orlando Hamilton.

STYLES

Top far left This isolepis grass looks well in a sleek metal container, with a trim of small slate pieces to keep the compost moist.

Bottom far left Another isolepis looks like a shaving brush emerging from its trim of small marble chippings.

Middle far left Like a piece of living sculpture, the partridge-breasted aloe has white flecks that reflect the white scheme.

Left Phalaenopsis orchids in stylish black and white containers bring a coolly understated elegance to any setting.

LUXURIOUS
MINIMALISM

Simplicity is the main aspect of this Zen-like approach to interior design. Its influence on the Western approach to creating a home is far-reaching.

The minimalist message is: keep only what is essential and elegant; clear out the clutter. The result will be a calm, harmonious living space.

This ideal would seem to rule out using plants for decoration, yet this is exactly the environment where a stunning plant like the moth orchid (*Phalaenopsis*) can make a luxurious contribution to a room. Its narrow stems allow light to filter through and its style is no-frills elegance. The wing-like shape of its beautiful blooms is responsible for its name, and also its visual appeal, since its sprays arch enticingly for most of the year. It likes the sun, but not too bright; and dislikes a draught. Ideal for a centrally heated environment, the moth orchid will flower as long as it is watered once a fortnight. Too much water upsets it, so do not saturate its epiphytic orchid compost.

Choose a container that will echo the slender lines of this plant. A smooth, satin-like surface would reflect the soft texture of its blooms; a tall container is best for a full-grown specimen. Oriental-style pots – either in highly lacquered or matt ceramic finishes – are an excellent choice, since they reflect the minimalist mood. Arrange the containers in a group to make a theatrical statement: a confident line of identical orchids or stiff-leaved plants – aloes or sansevierias, perhaps – parading along a windowsill or table top will strike the right note for disciplined minimalism.

Add a second indulgent note with interesting foliage. The ornamental grass *Isolepis cernua* (sometimes called *Scirpus*) is a pert little number with thread-like leaves in a tuft. Water every three weeks to keep in top condition. It looks cool in a modern metallic container.

Succulents work well in this environment, too. Partridge-breasted aloe (*Aloe variegata*) makes a striking display and is a good low-maintenance choice.

Top far right Strong and beautifully shaped, the imposing fiddle-leaf fig makes a strong impact against a sandblasted brick wall.

Middle far right The dark metallic bloom of this bat flower lends a contemporary edge to the grouping.

Bottom far right The bold and sturdy foliage of this dracaena adjacent to spiky mother-in-law's tongues creates a fascinating contrast.

Right The proliferation of colour in the paintings and carvings gives the indoor gardener freedom to use a myriad of pots and plants.

LIVING WITH
MODERN ART

A work of art makes its own definite statement in a room and any indoor plant has to have its own strong personality to compete for attention.

Whether the art is Renaissance, Impressionist, a framed modern print or poster, a bronze sculpture, or a tribal piece, the work is really the catalyst for the type of plant to suit the room. You can be inspired by a colour or a shape in a work of art. Try to reflect that design element in the plant that you choose.

Some plants are brilliant "biosculptures" and fit into an art-filled room with ease. For an urban jungle scene like this one (right), choose plants that echo the shapes in the tribal carvings. The largest plant here is the magnificent fiddle-leaf fig (*Ficus lyrata*). The mother-in-law's tongue (*Sansevieria trifasciata* 'Laurentii') has fierce, sword-like leaves, while the begonias (rex-cultorum types) have great patterned foliage and add to the jungle feel. These are all easily available, familiar plants, given a fresh look by the setting and the containers. More unusual is the metallic-coloured bat flower plant (*Tacca chantrierei*), which adds a hip urban look to a loft-style environment.

A vibrant canvas that dominates a room requires a lush plant with a comparably vibrant-coloured flower; a room with a collection of smaller, Impressionist-style paintings, on the other hand, might call for a group of smaller plants, perhaps planted in traditional ceramic jardinières. Contemporary prints and posters may suit eye-catching, spiky plants with boldly variegated foliage and lots of small but elegant coloured flowers.

The riot of colour in the paintings in the room shown right is repeated in the brightly patterned containers, which have been hand-painted to complement the artworks (see pages 106–7 for advice on painting pots). This is a fun, relaxed plant collection, with the accent very much on bold, tough foliage.

Note: Always use saucers under containers to protect the floor surface. Use deep saucers when you are going away for a few days since they hold more water.

Top far left The foliage of a Boston fern introduces both freshness and softness in this subtle, restrained interior.

Middle far left The fiery ornamental fruits of chilli peppers (*Capsicum annum*) make a witty design statement.

Bottom far left Standing sentinel by the French doors in a stylish container is a bold and exotic dracaena.

Left Pots of wonderful chilli peppers in front of a winter fire are a clever way of providing colour and texture.

BOLD AND
CONTEMPORARY

Modern homes can be bland, so design accessories in clever ways to create a personal look that reflects your way of life.

The move to open-plan living doesn't just produce a clean-lined interior; it also provides opportunities to make a plant display that reflects your personality. Plants come into their own when given lots of light and space, so you can have fun choosing the variety that is best for each location you have in mind.

In an interior dominated by clean lines, pale walls, and light floors, the mood is understated. Any plant has to have a similar presence – its role is to be colourful, to lift the mood, and to introduce texture. Containers should echo the smooth lines of the furniture, and in this case (left), the contemporary style of the fireplace.

Electric or acid-green foliage will lift neutrals or cool pastel hues like pale blue. Take the bright green, jagged foliage of the Boston fern (*Nephrolepsis exaltata* 'Bostoniensis'); although this gracefully drooping variety was raised in Boston over a century ago, if you place it in a classic white ceramic pot on a stylish timber table top, it will fit into a contemporary interior with ease. The fern will grow to about 1m (3ft) high and is spreading, too, so you may like to consider moving it when it is fully grown and replace it with a younger specimen.

The ornamental chilli pepper (*Capsicum annum*) grows to about 30cm (12in) tall, and bears star-shaped white flowers followed by numerous fruits, usually in bright red and yellow. These are an inspired and witty choice, especially when placed in very chic, pastel-coloured tubs. For the best growing conditions, place them in full light on a window sill.

Striking and exotic, a dracaena (*Dracaena fragrans* Deremensis Group) is at home in the light and is enough of an individual not to need grouping with other plants. Avoid direct summer sun and feed once every four weeks for strong growth.

ASIAN
FUSION STYLE

From the first trade in silks and porcelain to the current popularity of Feng Shui,
Asian design has long had an influence on homes in Europe and America.

The fusion of Eastern and Western style creates environments where orchids come into their own. By this, I am not referring to the almost ubiquitous white phalaenopsis, but to the richer-coloured varieties now emerging that incorporate the colours of Chinese porcelain with the simple lines of traditional Japanese furnishings.

Consider resonant and dramatic orchids such as odontoglossums – some of which are scented and give off a wonderful fragrance if placed near a seating area – or oncidiums, with their delicate flowers that resemble floating angels with wings, or even *Vuylstekeara* Cambria 'Plush', with its intricately detailed flowers. The vibrancy of these orchids chimes perfectly with the rich colours we commonly associate with the East and contrasts with the cooler tones of Western interiors.

Orchids have much to recommend them as flowering houseplants, since they flower for anything up to eight weeks. Furthermore, orchids are low-maintenance and require watering no more than once or twice a week. The secret to keeping your orchids healthy is to make sure that they never sit in water and to drain off any excess immediately to allow oxygen to get to their roots. Most orchids are long-lived plants that carry on flowering year on year if properly cared for.

Displaying orchids in lacquered or crackle-glazed containers is usually very effective: it makes them look more opulent while at the same time suits the Eastern theme. Another way to enhance the look is with the use of clean, strong, green plants like bamboo and grasses such as *Isolepis cernua*. The small indoor bamboo (*Pogonatherum saccharoideum*) in a bamboo bowl (see far right) is a very successful combination, but for height and a more architectural statement tall bamboo plants could be used, which can be further brought to life by spotlighting (see pages 110–17).

Top far left A grouping of individual lavender plants in flower, interspersed with small buckets of shells.

Middle far left Shells evoke summer days past, either used as a decorative trim or just simply displayed in baskets or containers.

Bottom far left This echeveria has been planted in a tall tin pot and decorated with twigs topped by tiny shells.

Left A cluster of silvery succulents brings a lived-in look to a summer beach house; stone and shell trims were found on the seashore.

BACK TO
NATURE

Stone, smooth pebbles, shells, and driftwood timber are desirable elements when creating an environment far away from hard-edged industrialization.

Creating a natural look inside with plants means applying simple criteria to your plant choices. Does it look as if it could have been transplanted from outside? Are its foliage and flowers soft and colourful in a country style? Is it low-maintenance? The choice of plants is wide-ranging, from alpine succulents to cottage garden varieties. For delicacy you can't go wrong with the aptly named falling stars or Italian bellflower (*Campanula isophylla*), trailing its delicate lilac, blue, or white flowers from small, pale-green foliage.

Fragrance is an important part of this concept and another delicate-looking plant, lavender (*Lavandula*), will provide this as long as it is given lots of light and is fed and watered regularly. What could be more natural?

Flaming Katy (*Kalanchoe*) is a compact, shrub-like succulent with interesting leaves; it produces dense flower heads from winter through to summer. Another favourite

succulent is the pretty echeveria (*Echeverea secunda* var. *glauca* 'Gigantea'). Stems of red and yellow flowers strike out of rosettes of divine blue-grey fleshy leaves in early summer, making the plant a talking point.

Seasonal colour is another point to consider if you want to create a natural effect. In winter, choose foliage that shines, and in spring go for masses of small flowers to bring a touch of sunshine inside.

The surfaces of pots and containers are key to a successful natural look. Tin containers with a weathered country patina, stone pottery jugs, rustic baskets, old terracotta pots decorated with sea shells or hand-painted in quiet, calm colours are the answer. Choose a pot that is in proportion with the size of the plant for the best visual effect. Try to combine a soft-looking plant with a pot that has a softer finish. Avoid highly finished pots — they are simply not natural.

Top far right Like
a platoon of soldiers,
this collection of desert
cacti stand to attention
following the line of
a dividing wall.

Middle far right Cactus
spines emerge from
areoles. These are also
the points from which
new stems and flowers
are produced.

Bottom far right Use
a heavy pot for tall cacti
and succulents, so they
don't overbalance. A
trim of stone chippings
adds further weight.

Right Lofty modern
rooms and large
succulents are made for
each other. Here, a tall
euphorbia is partnered
by a younger specimen.

INSPIRED BY
ARCHITECTURE

Architects like to push the limits of domestic construction and are a continuing
positive influence on the way we use room space.

Space is the ultimate luxury today, and when it is architect-designed it is maximized. In an open-plan interior like this, where there are few walls, a row of strong plants can help to define zones by acting as room dividers.

Cool, clean lines set the design agenda and enable the living spaces to be galleries for sculptural plants worthy of singular attention. For urban chic, go no further than eye-catching cacti. A valuable design feature and a living sculpture, cacti are also low-maintenance. Their solid green forms are shown off to best advantage when positioned against a clean white backdrop. They are survivors, virtually indestructible, and can get by on little water. For best results, however, regular watering (once every week or two) and feeding in summer (to encourage flowers) is advisable. Try to keep the collar of the plant dry.

It's worth investing in a tall specimen for sensational impact. Be sure to buy an appropriate pot, too – tall plants ought to live in containers chosen in proportion to the plant. Think big, bold, and simple. Natural textures are best for these plants; anything too decorative or ornate is overshadowed by the plant itself.

Take care where you place cacti – if they have spines (these grow directly from the stem and can be sharp), they can give a painful prick if brushed against or touched.

There is a black succulent, *Aeonium*, which looks fantastic in hard-edged environments. Add to the look by placing it in a smooth concrete container, making sure it has good drainage (see pages 120–21).

Cacti and succulents prefer sunshine all year for growth, yet in winter, when they are almost dormant, they like it cooler and do not need as much watering – if the plant is in a heated room, water it about once a month. They do not require feeding during the winter.

Top far left Olive trees are instant reminders of summers spent in the Mediterranean – or Florida, Israel, and other olive-growing lands.

Bottom far left Bougainvillea flowers themselves are inconspicuous but are surrounded by brilliantly coloured bracts.

Middle far left Terracotta is perfect for this style – look for old, weathered specimens in flea markets and antique shops.

Left Citrus and olive trees and bougainvillea sit happily by French windows, ready to step outside in warm weather.

MODERN
MEDITERRANEAN

The undeniable charm of sun-baked Mediterranean countries is frequently recreated in interiors throughout the world.

One of the most striking features of the Mediterranean landscape is the luscious bright pink or deep purple tracts of bougainvillea climbing and tumbling over whitewashed walls in their rush to sunbathe. Commonly known as the paper flower, its blooms are see-through; its stems are woody and spiky. *Bougainvillea glabra* is the basic species, but its hybrids, such as *B.* 'Alexander', which puts on a brilliant crimson display through summer to autumn, are more widely grown.

Try combining bougainvillea with hibiscus (*Hibiscus rosa-sinensis*) for its brightly coloured, magnificent trumpet-like flowers that last just a day or so. Lavish tender loving care on one and it can flower from spring to late summer (see pages 120–29 for care and maintenance). Trim it back from time to time if it threatens to get out of hand. For a reliable winter and spring side-show, add pots of poison primrose (*Primula obconica*) in a similar tone of pink or a contrasting white. Place in bright sun and do not overwater.

Choose plants that enjoy warmth and light, such as the olive (*Olea europea*), or calamondin (*Citrus mitis*), or the round kumquat (*Fortunella japonica*). At ground level, try Jerusalem cherry (*Solanum pseudocapiscum*), with its autumn and winter fruits that are effective imitation oranges (don't be tempted to eat them, as they are poisonous). For scent as well as show, choose a small lemon tree, or scented-leaved geranium (*Pelargonium* 'Fragrans') or the bushy, lemon-scented rose geranium, *Pelargonium* 'Graveolens'. A row of these on a sunny windowsill will remind you of those lazy days spent in the Med. The rising heat will release their essential oils.

To set the mood, non-plant elements are essential – terracotta pots, as long as they are distressed, reclaimed, or recycled and have an interesting patina, created by salts leaching through the material. Mosaic-decorated pots work well, too. Keep away from the glossy, just-out-of-the-garden-centre finish of brand new pots.

Top far right The baked-earth hues provide a moody backdrop for this variegated croton.

Middle far right African textiles in warm tones add to the safari look. Take full advantage of your holidays abroad to add to your collection.

Bottom far right Juxtaposing plants with contrasting foliage ensures a strong look.

Right A striking zebra plant and a philodendron trained on a moss pole are the finishing touches that brings this African-style setting to life for me.

AFRICAN
SAFARI STYLE

Tribal masks, multi-coloured textiles, and animal-skin prints are all part of a design trend that is firmly established in Western design vernacular.

Having spent my adolescence in West Africa, it gives me great pleasure to see these plants add the defining touch to an African-influenced interior. For me, Africa is about deep, burnt colours and rough textures, and this theme demands plants that create visual surprises at every turn in a room.

This selection of houseplants could be considered kitsch in another location, but they are absolutely appropriate for my African-style setting. The aptly named compact zebra plant (*Aphelandra squarrosa* 'Dania'), with its ivory-veined green leaves, is dramatic against evocative dark African timber, especially when its fantastic bright yellow flowers burst on to the scene. It is greedy, soaking up water when in a growth cycle, but needing little when it is dormant, and pernickety – it dislikes draughts and too much sun.

The sensational blushing philodendron (*Philodendron erubescens* 'Red Emerald') is a glossy-leaved, vigorous climber originally from the rainforest. Its height and presence give it enormous visual impact and, because of its size, it requires good support. Even more vibrant is the gleaming, almost leathery foliage of the tropical croton (*Codiaeum variegatum*) which has red, orange, purple, yellow, and green veins on its shiny leaves. It prefers a warm, humid environment but can be vulnerable to pests such as red spider mite and scale (see page 128).

Choose either beaten copper or sturdy patterned stone and ceramic containers for these large, exotic plants. Dark colours work best when the plant itself is dramatic. With tall plants, consider the weight of the container, as this needs to balance the weight of the plant. For compact plants, a simple style that allows the plant to take centre stage is best.

To clean glossy leaves, wipe carefully with a soft damp cloth or cotton balls. Soft new leaves should be left alone until they are firm, as they damage easily.

Top far left The jewel-like berries of the nertera are echoed in the colourful and shimmering beaded pot covers.

Bottom far left The arching umbrella effect of this cyperus, with its long grassy leaves, provides an exotic touch.

Middle far left Metallic elements are at the heart of this style; match their shine with glossy leaves and jewel-bright flowers.

Left The exotic shape of the scutellaria's red blooms suit the warm, rich mood a Moroccan look demands.

THE ROAD TO
MOROCCO

From beaten copper, colourful textiles, and embroidered silk slippers to decorative brass ornaments, the design influence of this North African country is eternal.

To capture the feel of a sensual Moroccan-style interior, the ideal planting scheme should feature lush foliage spiked with colourful flowers. Plants like this scutellaria (*Scutellaria costaricana*) add a touch of authentic spiciness – its small clusters of deep orange-red flowers burst through deep green foliage and are fabulous against a red-ochre wall, or on a tiled floor. Plants that create a heady, almost seductive atmosphere best reflect the style.

Consider exotic plants that reflect the sensuality in a North African-style room. Plants with glossy foliage and small vibrantly coloured flowers are evocative of Moroccan finery. Lushness comes with plants like the rush, *Cyperus involucratus*, also known as the umbrella plant, which adds texture with its glamorous, arching foliage. Its elegant straight stems grow to about 60cm (24in) high, and are topped with a burst of smaller fluffy leaves. For a shorter variety, try the selected form 'Gracilis' at no more than 30cm (12in) tall.

The great things about these plants is they are hard to kill. You cannot over-water them. They like bright light and regular warmth, but are hardy and quite able to survive cool winters if necessary.

More exotic enhancement is provided by the gorgeous bead-like fruits on the nertera plant (*Nertera granadensis*). Its dense mat of springy, creeping green leaves is covered in a mass of tiny orange berries, as small as *petit pois*. It puts on a great show during its late summer season of a few months. You may want to replace it when its red berries wither, since it is hard to coax back into bloom.

Favourite North African colours include turquoise, cobalt blue (believed to ward off evil spirits), and yellow, so choose containers in these colours. Brass and gold are also typical, so look for pots with lots of lustre. Mosaic patterns are ideal for decorative containers, or try winding strings of coloured beads around plant pots.

Top far left Scented plants make a good alternative to cut flowers. Here I used a grouping of gardenia and jasmine in small pots.

Middle far left Fragrant roses displayed adjacent to lily-of-the-valley create a scented corner in the room.

Bottom far left Bridal wreath can make a romantic centrepiece on a console in an entrance hall, producing a welcoming fragrance.

Left Groupings of delicate flowers, like these lily-of-the-valley and roses, complement soft, light-coloured schemes.

THE NEW
ROMANTICS

Romance has been part of the design vocabulary since we discovered softness, comfort, colour, and sensual textures are seductive.

Fragrance is a key element in creating a romantic mood, and roses, with their potent sentimental associations, are a natural choice. Choose full-bloomed varieties with larger flower-heads in soft colours for impact. Believe it or not, roses (*Rosa*) are often easier to care for than you might think. Make sure that you deadhead when see you signs of brown on the petals (see page 128).

Lily-of-the-valley (*Convallaria majalis*) has delicate, white, bell-shaped flowers that produce a sweet, heavy fragrance. I love them in miniature cream-coloured containers, grouped together, when they simply ooze sophistication with their hypnotic scent. In France, they are highly prized – on May 1, it is traditional to send them to loved ones as a token of affection. Although they are seasonal and only last a few weeks, their scent is not to be missed.

The gardenia (*Gardenia jasminoides*) is possessed of a sublime perfume and is a fantastic choice, combining luxuriance with fragrance. But it is temperamental and needs watering carefully with soft water (see pages 122–23). Sporting dark green leaves year-round, it produces superb waxy white flowers in summer.

Jasmine (*Jasminum polyanthum*), with its wispy shoots, also has a divine fragrance and sets a romantic tone, as does bridal wreath (*Stephanotis floribunda*). This twines into a wreath shape with training and pruning, and produces waxy white flowers whose fragrance fills the room and lifts the spirit.

Pots and containers should echo the romantic theme: china jardinières with interesting decorative designs are ideal, as is any pot with a smooth surface finish. Pale colours are best – cream, white, pink, lilac, or blue – although you could substitute a modern container with a glossy black finish to provide a stronger contrast to exotic-looking blooms.

Top far left Tall umbrella grass in a stylish metallic container echoes the line of the pillar in this modern loft, yet softens its stark textures.

Middle far left Temper the sharpness of the agave by putting moss on top of the compost in the pot (and spray with water from time to time to keep it green).

Bottom far left The peace lily needs light when flowering, so I move it near a window on a clear winter's day. It should not sit in full sun.

Left A feathery grass is positioned next to spiky agave in shiny metal containers on a polished wooden floor for a striking, high-tech effect.

STYLISH STATEMENTS

High-tech homes, where there is a fusion of the latest materials and cutting-edge design, call for smart plant choices.

Modern, clean-lined interiors can act as a gallery and are a good place to show off plants with star quality – those with large, bold leaves and thick, sculptural foliage. For a really unusual effect, the Mexican elephant's foot or pony tail (*Beaucarnea recurvata*) is impressive and low-maintenance. It has a wide stem and a wild-looking topknot of arching leaves (hence the common name). It requires a large and deep container to suit its woody, bulbous base. Like the African fiddle-leaf fig (*Ficus lyrata*), with its boldly veined glossy leaves, and elephant's ear (*Alocasia x amazonica*), with its dramatic white-veined, dark green foliage, it is also a good choice for a contemporary space.

Similarly attention-grabbing is the umbrella plant (*Cyperus albostriatus*), with reedy stems and drooping, thread-like leaves that waft in the air, bringing movement and a sense of life to the room; these grow from 20cm (8in) to 2.5m (8ft) tall. This is a plant that likes to have its feet in water, so make sure that it never dries out.

Or opt for tall pennisetum, which is a graceful type of ornamental grass. Although not a conventional houseplant, it works when you have floor-to-ceiling windows which provide it with the optimum light it needs. Pennisetum prefers its roots permanently wet and benefits from spraying with a mist of water where the air is dry (for instance, in an air-conditioned or centrally heated room). Combine pennisetum with the silvery grey tones of the architectural *Agave americana* and you have an exceptional double act.

Grouping definite forms around an expanse of floor-to-ceiling windows adds another visual dimension, walls are dissolved, and the outside appears to merge with the interior. When the weather warms up in summer, the plants could step outside (provided the pots are weather-proof), and effectively become dual-purpose decorations. Remember to bring them inside again if the temperature plummets at night.

Top far right Glazed ceramic containers are great for complementing the kalanchoe's small but charming retro flowers.

Middle far right Funky 1970s glazed pots are ideal for plants with glossy leaves.

Bottom far right Place trailing spider plants against acrylic mirror wall bubbles and create instant plant chic.

Right Houseplants are the essential touch if you want to recreate that authentic 1970s vibe.

HOUSEPLANT
REVIVAL

Plants that were popular when flared trousers and acrylic furniture were in style are making a showy comeback, with help from the retro movement.

Retro style is bold and imaginative, often achieved with vibrant colour and strong lines. Not for the faint-hearted, some of the retro plants have flowers in shades of red, bright yellow, and acid-orange, with, of course, the deep green of the foliage.

Pots of Kalanchoe (flaming Katy) are perfect retro plants, bringing with them a sense of 1970s style that some of us might like to forget (along with bell-bottoms and tank tops), but for a younger generation it is new and uncharted territory. These flowering succulents (usually unnamed hybrids, with red, white, yellow, or pink flowers) are great for people who are away from home a lot, because they don't need a lot of watering and tolerate a certain amount of benign neglect. These plants can grow to about 30cm (12in) tall, and will flower for months on end. Look also at its close relative, Kalanchoe daigremontiana (the Devil's backbone), which can grow up to 90cm (36in) and has an abundance of fringed leaves. These plants used in groupings are a great way to achieve a chic designer look on the cheap.

On a larger scale, the delightfully familiar *Monstera deliciosa* (known as the Swiss cheese plant because of its holed, glossy leaves) is at home in any corner as long as it has the support of a bamboo cane or something similar.

The return of pert plastic and acrylic furniture also opens up a window of opportunity for cute plants such as the spider plant, *Chlorophytum comosum* 'Vittatum', with its cascading stems and tiny white flowers. It is a low-maintenance plant though too much heat and not enough light will leave it looking pale and wan. Its partner in style-crime is *Crassula ovata*, known as the jade plant. The Chinese, following a Feng Shui tradition, put it in the window to entice good fortune, hence it is also called the money plant. Both of these need a splash of water from time to time, and in winter make sure that they do not dry out.

COLOUR

SCENT

CHOOSING
SCENTED PLANTS

Scented rooms have an invaluable place in our sensory vocabulary, reminding us of magical moments, revived when we encounter a similar aroma.

Throughout our lives we all build up a memory bank of fragrant associations, and it is to your personal "library" of scents that you should turn when deciding which houseplants will be perfect in a room.

When deciding where to place a fragrant plant, look at the seating area. It would be a shame to place it away from where you sit most of the time. Sitting it on a table adjacent to a sofa is perfect for enjoying the fragrance at close quarters, so is a table that you pass several times a day, since you get to smell the fragrance on each occasion.

Each plant has a signature fragrance, and for it to be fully appreciated it requires space. Placing two or three competing fragrances together is detrimental to the power of each and confuses the senses.

Also, consider the size of the room. Plants with a powerful fragrance are overwhelming in a small room, while in a large traditional drawing room or modern loft space you may find that you need several containers of the same plant placed around the room to really appreciate their scent.

FRESH SCENTS

Plants that produce refreshing, uplifting aromas that add a fresh note are easy to grow in the right conditions. The following plants are worth considering:

- In the kitchen: sweet basil (*Ocimum basilicum*) – rub the leaves together for an instant fragrance hit. Lemon-scented thyme (*Thymus x citriodorus* 'Aureus') is bushy, with fresh lemon-scented, golden-green leaves. A mint bush (*Prostanthera rotundifolia*) – each time you brush by it, a minty aroma is released from its leaves.
- Some pelargoniums are well-known for their scented leaves. Try, for instance, *P.* 'Fragrans', *P.* 'Lady Plymouth', or *P.* 'Old Spice'.
- Narcissi – tazetta narcissi (*Narcissus* hybrids) have beautiful cream flowers in late autumn through to spring, and like a warm place in the sun. Use these to bring a sense of early spring inside.

HEADY SCENTS

Rich scents always promote a sense of well-being. Indulge your senses with some of the following heady houseplants:
- Hyacinths (*Hyacinthus orientalis* hybrids) are glorious. Their distinct fragrance is superb in late winter and spring.
- Gardenias (*Gardenia augusta* cultivars) are showy plants with large, double creamy white flowers in summer and autumn, and give off a divine exotic fragrance.
- Easter lilies (*Lilium longiflorum*) grow to 90cm (36in) and produce very fragrant trumpet-shaped flowers in warm and moderately humid conditions.
- Miniature irises (*Iris reticulata*) grow to 15cm (6in) high and bear fragrant flowers in late winter.

Top right The rich golden hue of sweet-smelling tazetta narcissi.

Top far right A small citrus produces delightful fresh scents, and fruit for a gin and tonic without even moving outside.

Bottom right The waxy blooms of the gardenia are richly fragrant.

Bottom far right Tubular bells of a bridal wreath about to burst open.

Other fragrant plants
Lily-of-the-valley *Convallaria majalis*
Grape hyacinth *Muscari armeniacum*
Rosemary *Rosmarinus officinalis*
Chocolate plant *Cosmos atrosanguineus*
Odontoglossum hybrids
Jasmine *Jasminum polyanthum*

MAKING
COLOUR CHOICES

Creating the ambience in a room requires an understanding of how colour influences moods. With houseplants, we can use nature as the inspiration.

Colour stimulates the creative senses, and can provide enormous emotional satisfaction. Looking at the sunlight filtering through a delicate tulip petal can be a breathtaking experience that will remain locked in your memory for ever. Personality affects colour preferences. To some people, only a brilliant red can satisfy, bringing vibrancy and vitality to a colour scheme; to others the palest shade of cream is perfect. It is important to work out the colours to which you are instinctively drawn, and those about which you are ambivalent.

MATCHING COLOURS

Observe how nature matches colours – it combines foliage, which ranges in colour from green through to silvery grey, with white, yellow (the buttercup being the brightest example), orange, red, blue, purple, lilac – right through the colour wheel. Here are just a few examples of nature's talent for matching colours:

- White, cream, and a hint of palest yellow. These are "cool" colours, which when grouped together create a sophisticated effect in any setting. They have a purity that is peaceful, almost spiritual, matched by no other colour in the spectrum.
- Blue, pale blue, and a hint of lilac. Each of these colours is from a similar segment of the spectrum and flowers in any of these shades will produce a calming effect when displayed together.

- Red, pink, and a hint of pale orange. Warm colours within the same "family" have an inviting ambience that brings vitality into a plant selection.
- Yellow and gold. Strong colours such as these have a powerful impact in a room, and can look fabulous when plants are grouped en masse.
- Green. The basic colour of all plant leaves, this always has a calming effect. Mix different shades together to create a rich but restful picture.

CLASHING COLOURS

Some colours shout out loud when combined, giving the senses a disturbing jolt. The following are some examples of what not to put together:

- Red and blue flowers. The red will detract from the vibrancy of the deep blue and vice versa. Each is bold and beautiful in its own right; there is no need to mix them. Purple flowers are also best kept away from red and blue.
- Yellow and deep purpley black flowers as seen in some of the more innovatively bred tulips. The sight of the two together offends almost immediately.
- Purple and orange flowering plants. Vibrant colours, yes, but one will fight the other for attention if they are placed near each other.

Again, the rules for combining colour are personal, and what I think clashes may look like heaven to you. Common sense generally prevails.

Top right The elegant white flower of the luscious peace lily.

Top far right For sheer beauty, look no further than the delicate flowers of an orchid.

Bottom right The pale variegated foliage of a dieffenbachia is striking.

Bottom far right The florists' classic, cyclamen is still my favourite, despite the trend for more extraordinary plants.

Wonderful whites
Begonia *Begonia x tuberhybrida* (white varieties)
Paper flower *Bougainvillea* (white varieties)
Citrus *Citrus*
Lily-of-the-valley *Convallaria majalis*
Gardenia *Gardenia augusta*
Hyacinth *Hyacinthus orientalis* (white varieties)

Pretty pinks

Begonia *Begonia x tuberhybrida*
(pink varieties)

Paper flower *Bougainvillea*
(pink varieties)

Cyclamen *Cyclamen persicum*
(pink varieties)

Amaryllis *Hippeastrum*
(pink varieties)

Hyacinths *Hyacinthus orientalis*
(pink varieties)

Hydrangea *Hydrangea
macrophylla*

Bottom far left Pretty In pink – the waxy bloom on the leaves of this succulent echeveria have a pronounced rosy tinge.
.

Bottom left The delicately fragrant, tubular flowers of tropical bouvardias are carried in dainty, posy-like clusters.

Bottom right This tillandsia, a bromeliad from the Peruvian Amazon, has intriguing, shrimp-pink flowers.

Bottom far right The beautifully marked, pewter-grey leaves of this urn plant are the perfect foil to the luminous pink flowers.

Left The brilliant green fronds of an upright Boston fern.

Top right Crowns of delicate, feathery leaves top the reed-like stems of the umbrella plant.

Top far right Standing proud, the leathery leaves of the mother-in-law's tongue are boldly edged with yellow and banded with zebra-like stripes.

Bottom right The silvery green leaves of this succulent aloe have distinctive toothed edges.

Bottom far right The maidenhair fern is a mass of soft green foliage.

Gorgeous greens
Bird's nest fern *Asplenium nidus*
Hard fern *Blechnum* species
Tree ivy *Fatshedera lizei*
Weeping fig *Ficus benjamina*
Kentia palm *Howea fosteriana*
Isolepis cernua
Swiss cheese plant *Monstera deliciosa*
Blushing philodendron
  Philodendron erubescens

Far left Leaves as well as flowers can provide colour. The spiny, fleshy, glaucous blue leaves of this aloe are a long-term attraction, perfectly offset by the granite chippings.

Top left Hyacinths have a powerful scent that matches the depths of their colours – in this case, a rich purplish blue.

Bottom left This hydrangea has flowers of an intense electric blue, offset by white centres.

Beautiful blues

Campanula carpatica
Falling stars *Campanula isophylla*
Echeveria **species**
Bluebell *Hyacinthoides non-scripta*
Lavender *Lavandula*
Rosemary *Rosmarinus officinalis*
African violet *Saintpaulia*

COLOUR SCHEMES

The colour scheme of a room also has a bearing on the colours you decide upon for houseplants. Good advice from experts is to start with a favourite colour and choose a group of similar hues that work with it. Experiment with smaller inexpensive plants first, before making that exuberantly colourful choice. A living room with white walls and pale flooring cries out for a splash of colour – sometimes not present even in the furniture and soft furnishings. In such a scheme, an interesting tall, elegant plant with exotic foliage and a shot of colour in its blooms can add enormous impact. As can a group of smaller plants in one colour – perhaps four or five pots of purple hyacinths on a tray in the middle of the table.

FOLIAGE COLOUR

Colourful foliage, too, is impressive in its own quiet way. There are quite a few choices: purple and white, almost black, variegated green and yellow, subtle shades of green (as seen in the ubiquitous maidenhair fern, page 43) and that gorgeous silvery grey with red of the ornamental cabbage (right). Some foliage is magically in two shades, the top of the leaf being one shade, the underside in another shade entirely, for instance the peacock plant (*Stromanthe* 'Stripestar') which has a dark green leaf decorated by a pale green midrib, and a dark purple underside.

Top far left The African violet used to be thought of as an old lady's plant, but the younger generation should also consider its charms.

Bottom far left The closest to a "black" plant, the ophiopogon has leaves that are always a talking point.

Top left All rex begonias have brilliant leaves, with a pronounced metallic sheen. The flowers are inconspicuous and can be removed if you wish.

Bottom left Ornamental cabbages produce their best colours as the temperature dips in winter – but don't eat them!

Deep purples

Elephant's ear plant *Alocasia sanderiana*
Chilli pepper *Capsicum annuum*
Cyclamen *Cyclamen persicum* hybrids
Hyacinth *Hyacinthus orientalis* hybrids
Moth orchid *Phalaenopsis* hybrids
Poison primrose *Primula obconica*
Tradescantia pallida **'Purpurea'**
Wandering Jew *Tradescantia zebrina* **'Purpusii'**

Radical reds

Begonia *Begonia x tuberhybrida* (red varieties)

Paper flower *Bougainvillea* (red varieties)

Desert cacti (some species)

Chilli pepper *Capsicum annuum*

Cyclamen *Cyclamen persicum* (red varieties)

Rose of China *Hibiscus rosa-sinensis* (red varieties)

Amaryllis *Hippeastrum* (red varieties)

Flaming Katy *Kalanchoe*

Medinilla magnifica

Bottom far left At home in tropical Africa, gerberas have lipstick-red daisy-like flowers of unmatched vibrancy. Use them as the centrepiece of any grouping of plants.

Bottom left Not actually flowers – which are inconspicuous – the terminal bracts produced by the guzmania are as brilliant as any blossom.

Bottom right Scutellarias seem to have burst into flame when the intense scarlet flowers appear during summer.

Bottom far right You can hardly fail with clivias, one of the easiest of all flowering houseplants to grow. The vibrant orange and yellow flowers are reliably produced each spring.

Far left All crotons have dramatically marked foliage. This is the appropriately named 'Gold Star', which has leaves generously streaked and mottled with yellow.

Top left Tuberous begonias have flowers that can easily be mistaken for roses, as this rich golden-yellow variety amply demonstrates.

Bottom left Most kalanchoes have red or pink flowers, but recent breeding programmes have extended the colour range to include a brilliant yellow as illustrated here.

Mellow yellows
Zebra plant *Aphelandra squarrosa*
Desert cacti (some species)
Chilli pepper *Capsicum annuum*
Dracaena fragrans Deremensis Group
Transvaal daisy *Gerbera jamesonii* hybrids
Jerusalem cherry *Solanum pseudocapsicum*

SHAPE

PATTERN

TEXTURE

PLANT
PROPORTIONS

The question of size is paramount for both plant and container. One element must balance the other for harmony to be achieved.

The proportions of the room in which your chosen plant will be living are also a consideration. In a large room with high ceilings choose a tall plant with a real presence – nothing too spindly, but something exotic, such as the magnificent aloe (*Aloe vera*), which is a great personal favourite of mine, illustrated on the opposite page. Its strong, almost aggressive form and its dangerous-looking fleshy, textural leaves dictate the type of territory it requires: masses of space. Large plants emphasise the space in which they live; smaller plants provide a small-scale theatrical dimension. There are no rules other than keeping a sense of proportion.

PLACES FOR TALL PLANTS

The best places for tall plants are those which will benefit from the addition of a focal point. The more physical interest there is on a tall plant, the more it will need a platform for its splendour.

● A plain painted wall or a timber-panelled wall at the end of a medium- to large-sized room makes a great backdrop for tall, spiky plants whose foliage will stand out against the textural surface.

● Use tall plants as a room divider to hide a home office in the corner of a living room, or an exercise cycle area in a bedroom. Leafy plants give best coverage.

● For impact in an entrance hall place a specimen plant in a medium-lit corner.

● Set a group of several tall plants against large picture windows for good effect – they can even act as a privacy screen, obviating the need for curtains.

PLACES FOR SMALL PLANTS

Anywhere that cries out for a spot of colour or texture is good for small plants. For greater impact, group them in two's or three's, whether on a kitchen bench, tabletop, or the floor.

● If you want to display one sensational plant on a bedside table, choose a small one that won't easily be knocked over, and place it on the furthest side from the bed, so that it has space to grow out.

● Plants placed on the end of bookshelves can ramble and cascade down to the next shelf or beyond.

● In a small room, a luscious yet low-growing flowering plant on a side table adds elegance.

● Corners and hard-edged flat surfaces benefit from the softening effect of miniature ferns.

● Put one or two exotic little plants that like humidity on a steamy bathroom shelf or windowsill.

PLACES FOR COMPACT PLANTS

Small cacti are the most interesting compact plants, closely followed by other succulents of the aloe variety.

● Place several identical low-growing plants on a coffee table (with smart saucers under each plant).

Right The patina on this slate pot is a perfect complement to the matt aloe leaves. Placing three of these in a row in an open-planned room was a stroke of genius.

Tall plants
Dieffenbachia sanguine 'Exotica'
Euphorbia abyssinica
Weeping fig *Ficus benjamina*
Amaryllis *Hippeastrum* hybrids
Kentia palm *Howea fosteriana*
Swiss cheese plant *Monstera deliciosa*

Small plants
Desert cacti (young plants)
Falling stars *Campanula isophylla*
Cyclamen *Cyclamen persicum* hybrids
Flaming Katy *Kalanchoe* hybrids

● Put a group on a windowsill in any room. If it's in full sun, put them in the shade for the hottest period of the day and water as required.

PLACES FOR SPREADING PLANTS

Specimens that spread need lots of space around them, either so they don't get brushed as you walk by, causing damage, or so that their foliage doesn't become entangled with the plant next door. Climbers need things they can get their hooks into; trailers need wide open spaces to meander along.

● Centre stage on a mantelpiece or in an open display cabinet is a convenient spot for strong, broad-leaved foliage plants.

● A long ledge under a window, or above a bookshelf, is good for flowering plants with lots of foliage.

When choosing a container for any of these sizes, remember this golden rule: the plant ought to measure about one third of the final combination; two thirds is taken up by the container. Also, try to imagine how large the plant is going to grow – will it "grow into" its pot after a few weeks? If you don't want to look at the compost until it's covered by foliage, cover it with small white pebbles or even soft and sexy moss. This also helps to keep moisture in during the important early days.

Top far left This guzmania spreads as wide as it is tall, so site it where you can be sure you won't brush against it in passing.

Bottom far left These young barrel cacti, grouped together for maximum impact, are squat, compact plants that won't fall over easily – low-maintenance too!

Top left Slipper orchids are tall, elegant plants best seen in splendid isolation. Staking ensures that the slender flower stem won't keel over.

Bottom left Play with scale. Setting this diminutive rat's-tail cactus in an over-large planter lessens the chances of you catching your hands on its spines.

Compact plants
Aloe aristata
Partridge-breasted aloe *Aloe variegata*
Desert cacti (young plants)
Echeveria species
African violets *Saintpaulia* hybrids

Spreading plants
Urn plant *Aechmea fasciata*
Spider plant *Chlorophytum comosum* 'Vittatum'
Kentia palm *Howea fosteriana*
Medinilla magnifica
Boston fern *Nephrolepis exaltata* 'Bostoniensis'

EXPLOITING LEAF SHAPE

When a plant has extraordinary foliage it is a good long-term investment, since it will be a fabulous focal point throughout the year.

Dramatic effects can be achieved with foliage. The bigger and more extraordinarily shaped, the stronger the visual reaction. What is it about plants with great foliage that attracts us? For one thing, they emphasise the underlying philosophy that plants are an integral part of a room's design, not a last-minute addition to fill an empty space. They have splendid architectural form, complementing the clean lines in a room. Also, leaves are enticing – you want to touch them, smell them, and they give hours of visual pleasure. They can be small, large, soft, feather-like, furry, strong, oval, round, pointed, stand to attention like sentinels or arch, swoon, or squiggle in chaotic abandonment.

Leaves range in size and shape from the tiny foliage of mind-your-own business (*Soleirolia soleirolii*), to the larger creeping fig (*Ficus pumila*) and pilea leaves and some of the ivies (*Hedera*) and wandering Jew (*Tradescantia*), and lastly, to those in the super-leaf league, the fiddle-leaf fig (*Ficus lyrata*), mother-in-law's tongue (*Sansevieria trifasciata* 'Laurentii'), philodendron, and Swiss cheese plant (*Monstera deliciosa*).

For unique style, houseplants with narrow or sword-shaped foliage are fantastic. They are instant talking points and if used effectively can become the mainstay of a grouping on a floor or ledge. Narrow leaves add height, starring above a display of three or four plants of a more compact habit. In design terms, tall plants with narrow leaves break up the horizontal lines that form with such a grouping. Also, vertical leaves are essential for those narrow spaces for which you despaired of ever finding a suitable plant.

Large plant leaves are not necessarily on dominating plants, for instance the dumb cane (*Dieffenbachia seguine*) grows only to about a metre, but has leaves up to 45cm (18in) long. Depending on the variety, they can be liberally splashed or edged with creamy white or yellow. The Japanese aralia (*Fatsia japonica*) also has sensationally large leaves that spread open like fans, though in a container the plant is of only modest dimensions overall. This is the ideal choice for creating a focal point against a plain wall. It will amaze, as will crystal anthurium (*Anthurium crystallinum*), which is blessed with large, dark green, velvety leaves with prominent white veins.

Small plants also have their charms. Take the string of beads (*Senecio rowleyanus*), for one, which produces a collection of tiny, bead-like leaves hanging over the edge of the pot on fine threads.

Place contrasting leaf shapes together, mixing tall and short plants with a variety of habits, i.e. some that grow vertically with others that arch elegantly, or have a spreading habit.

Top right Most grasses have long, slender leaves. Those of this isolepis are thread-like and arch over like a filament lamp.

Top far right The bird's-nest fern has bright shiny green, wavy-edged fronds that curl over at the tips.

Bottom right The leaves of the false aralia are toothed like a chain saw.

Bottom far right Like peas in a pod, the leaves of the string of beads are almost perfectly spherical.

USING
PATTERN & TEXTURE

Many plants also have a tactile quality: any with textured leaves, or flowers, will complement your decor if you use them creatively.

Plants with soft, velvety foliage, broad-patterned leaves, or spectacular spines will become the focal point in a room, so it's advisable to use them in a theatrical way. Choose each plant for a specific purpose: if you want to make a fashion statement on a dining table, use a low-growing cactus or another variety of succulent with striking, broad leaves. It is vital that guests can see each other across the table. Set two or three containers in a shallow, clear acrylic container, top the compost with tiny white frosty chips of stone – voila! You may like to use pots of slender club-rush (*Isolepis cernua*) in a row, or the pretty mind-your-own-business (*Soleirolia soleirolii* 'Variegata') with its tiny silvered leaves forming a creeping carpet. Put these in small modern terracotta or metallic pots and you will have created a chic setting.

Some plants have everything, like the golden barrel cactus (*Echinocactus grusonii*). It's a round, prickly ball and has a masculinity about it which makes it perfect for a New Man in his urban, high-tech environment. Any of the agave tribe (particularly *A. victoriae-reginae*) and some kalanchoes (such as *K. thyrsiflora*) suit this environment, too.

If you want a specimen plant for a dull corner, look for something tall, leafy, and exotic. The lush Colombian rainforest plant crystal anthurium (*Anthurium crystallinum*) has large, dark green leaves patterned with white veins.

Their surface is smooth, like velvet in appearance. It requires high humidity and to be kept moist and out of the way of any draughts.

Choose plants with sex appeal; look for leaf texture – tough and glossy deep green, soft and covered in tiny hairs, studded with dangerous spikes, and wound in fine threads, red-tipped leaves, or just wild and wilful structures such as the corkscrew rush (*Juncus effusus* 'Spiralis'), whose tendrils wriggle all over the place.

For pattern, choose plants with dramatically veined leaves in cream or pink, variegated green and yellow or green and white broad leaves, or plants with speckled, striped, and rippled leaf effects. Wandering Jew or inch plant (*Tradescantia zebrina* 'Quadricolor') grows to about 25cm (10in) and it likes to wander everywhere it can, either down from a hanging basket or along from a container on a high shelf. Its green leaves are patterned with silver stripes and a hue of pink and red is visible, too.

The trusty tiger begonia (a rex-cultorum type) is a compact plant with dark foliage dotted with splashes of yellow and is just one of many begonias with flair. The painted-leaf begonia has lop-sided leaves shaded a deep, warm pink; others put on a silvery show, or purple, purple and red, red, green and pink... oh, and plain green.

Top right The corkscrew rush – obvious how it got its name, is it not?

Top far right Touchy-feely. The smooth, pewter-grey leaves of this kalanchoe are crying out to be fondled lovingly.

Bottom right In the wild, the spiny margins of the agave keep chomping animals at bay – so handle with care.

Bottom far right The roly-poly barrel cactus is barbarously armed with thick spines, sharp as needles, that shine luminous gold in sunlight.

Top far left The kris plant has dramatic, arrow-shaped leaves with silver veining and a pronounced metallic sheen.

Top left Blissfully easy to grow and seemingly at home anywhere, the wandering Jew has peppermint-striped leaves that positively gleam.

Bottom left 'Norah Bedson' is just one of a huge number of begonias that are grown for their strikingly marked leaves.

SITES

STATEMENTS
AT THE ENTRANCE

Very often a foyer or entrance hall is a bland, uninspiring place, so it is the ideal place for the type of plants that are welcoming and will add attitude.

An entrance hall creates the first impression, it is the link between the exterior and what is to come inside. So often halls are neglected because they're considered too narrow, too dark and, besides, you only pass through on the way to somewhere else.

Yet the hall is the vital introduction to your home, setting the style, and should be treated with respect. Architectural details are more apparent in halls, so complement these features with a cunning choice of plants.

IDEAS FOR HALLWAYS

In long, narrow halls where space is at a premium, choose compact plants with impact. The choice of display areas is limited, so use them imaginatively.

- Centre stage on a narrow console against the wall is perfect for foliage affairs, such as asparagus fern (*Asparagus setaceus* 'Nanus'), or plants that will bear small but gorgeous flowers or fruits, such as ornamental peppers (*Capsicum annum* 'Festival Orange').
- Choose a pot in similar colours to those on the wall or on the floor. It also should be of a medium size so it doesn't grab attention or look too big in the narrow space.
- In a more spacious area, you can be adventurous. A line of small pots acts as a trail from the front door, gently beckoning the visitor onwards and through to the rest of the house.

- Choose small plants with similar growth habits that will add a welcoming and colourful touch.
- The containers are important, too, especially if you want to create a trail. They really ought to be the same size and colour for a successful grouping. In the setting (left) I used small white ceramic pots that have a smooth glazed finish and are all identical. They are the perfect complement to the glossy white floor and stairs.

IDEAS FOR STAIRS

Usually, stairs are designed for practicality – moving up to another level. This often means there is not much spare space. They can be draughty, so you have to choose plants that like this situation.

- On narrow stairs with a landing halfway up, place a smart stool or plant holder from a second-hand store. Here you can display plants with medium spread or even trailers such as string of beads (*Senecio rowleyanus*) or wandering Jew (*Tradescantia fluminensis* 'Albovittata'). If the light levels are low, a fern can fit the bill.
- Containers full of bulbs such as crocuses put on a cheerful show and can be planted in the garden after they have flowered.
- Small containers placed to one side of each stair tread look fantastic. Choose plants such as cacti, a velvet-leaved kalanchoe, or the amazing slender club-rush (*Isolepsis cernua*) for effect.

Left This sentinel line of mind-your-own-business looks almost like a row of topiary specimens, bringing a touch of well-groomed class and sophistication to a simply conceived hallway.

Plants that put up with draughty places
Agave victoriae-reginae
Cast-iron plant *Aspidistra elatior*
Cacti (desert species)
Echeveria species
Weeping fig *Ficus benjamina*
Olive *Olea europea*
Mother-in-law's tongue
 Sansevieria trifasciata
 'Laurentii'

ARRANGEMENTS FOR
THE LIVING ROOM

The living room is the heart of a home, where friends are invited to relax and be entertained – and where plants are destined for display.

The decoration of your living space will determine the style demanded by the plants. The same rule applies whether it is a traditional room, an Art Deco space, or Victorian. Examine the features in your living room and take a lead from them – does one shape dominate? Is it purely colour and does it need a calming plant? Are the accessories textural and so require textural foliage to complement the look? The following are just a few ideas you should consider.

IDEAS FOR FAMILIES

Plants that can withstand a lot of activity around them, and occasional neglect, are ideal. Delicate flowers such as orchids are not suitable, and soft foliage will not stand much chance of survival in a family living room with a cat, dog, and children! If you have small children, be careful where you place any plants that have sharp, pointed leaves and spiny cacti.

- For shelves and windowsills, choose ferns with arching fronds such as the Boston fern (*Nephrolepsis exaltata* 'Bostoniensis') or bromeliads, such as blushing bromeliad (*Neoregelia coralinae* f. *tricolor*) with its dense, bold, shiny green leaves. In the flowering season, it produces an eye-catching red heart.
- Trailing plants look cool when placed on high display shelves. Out of the way of small hands, they can grow to their hearts' content.

IDEAS FOR MANTELS OVER FIREPLACES

- Miniature iris (*Iris reticulata*) has fragrant flowers in late winter and grows to about 15cm (6in).
- Fleshy succulents such as aloes and echeverias will thrive in the warm, dry air above the fireplace.
- Cacti like mantels and there are a lots to choose from. Look for similar shapes, and those that will produce flowers at the same time. Line up a range of heights from the left to right, tallest to smallest. Choose stylish containers for them as they will be prominent in the room.
- One showpiece makes a strong style statement. Choose a medium-sized plant that likes warmth and doesn't trail (no singed leaves). An amaryllis (*Hippeastrum*) is simply amazing, growing to about 50cm (20in). Its trumpet-shaped flowers burst forth in winter or spring.

IDEAS FOR OCCASIONS

- A wedding party at home requires miniature roses in tin or ceramic containers. Choose double petal varieties that will look exquisite grouped together on a table top or window sill. 'Cinderella' has double, silvery pink petals and a whiff of fragrance.
- Parties of any kind need dressing up. Plants with bold, interestingly shaped foliage, in unusual containers, are ideal. Take a large, shallow, clear perspex container, fill with bulb fire, add eight hyacinths (*Hyacinthus orientalis*) and cover the soil with tiny white stone chips. Easy, chic appeal.

Right Clivias are among the easiest of houseplants to grow and will produce a show of vivid orange-red flowers every spring. The simple beauty of the arching, leathery, shiny green leaves is not to be sniffed at either, and the whole plant contributes a cool elegance to this understated interior.

Plants that purify air
Spider plant *Chlorophytum comosum* 'Vittatum'
Dumb cane *Dieffenbachia seguine*
Dracaena fragrans **Deremensis Group**
Weeping fig *Ficus benjamina*
Rubber plant *Ficus elastica*
False aralia *Schefflera elegantissima*

Left For a touch of night-time glamour, these arum lilies are unsurpassed. The golden bowl of glass chippings in which they appear to be growing, together with the glass and chrome table, seem to reflect a halo of light around them.

Right By day the ensemble is equally sophisticated, but now the look is high tech and coolly elegant.

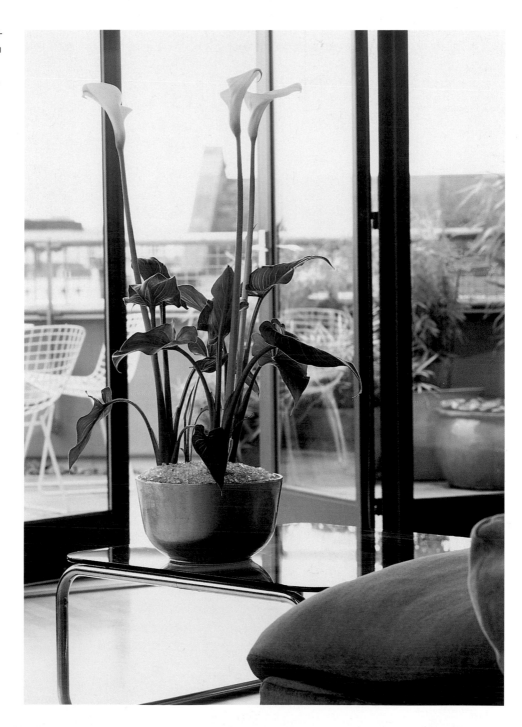

HERBS
IN THE KITCHEN

Kitchens are generally functional places, where the greenery that indoor plants bring is especially welcome: living herbs that can be used to liven up your cooking are the supremely practical choice.

In most households – whether urban or rural – the kitchen is one of the central rooms of the house. Generally warm and well-lit, it offers the ideal environment for growing culinary herbs. Besides adding distinction to your cooking, herbs also have valuable restorative qualities – as you can discover by running your fingertips along a thyme or rosemary plant to release the powerful aromatic oils – and a cup of chamomile tea makes an excellent nightcap at the end of a stressful day.

GROWING HERBS

I prefer to buy my herbs from a garden centre or nursery, as invariably supermarket-bought plants are on the spindly side, being intended to provide leaves for a few meals only. Strong-growing plants will provide leaves for much longer. Evergreens such as rosemary and bay can be used throughout winter. The green-fingered could try growing tender herbs such as basil and parsley from seed.

● Most herbs are best in a nutrient-low, fairly gritty compost that drains easily, apart from mint, which appreciates a damp growing medium.

● Keep herbs on a sunny windowsill. Open the window periodically to keep the air around them moving.

● Pinching out the growing tips from time to time produces compact, bushy plants.

● Mist over the plants every once in a while to keep them fresh and to release their evocative aroma.

STYLING IDEAS FOR CONTAINERS

The containers you choose should be suitable for herbs – most need good drainage – as well as reflecting the style of your kitchen.

● In a rustic kitchen, distressed terracotta pots are ideal. They can be painted to match the decor. Shallow troughs are particularly good for low-growing herbs such as thymes and marjoram.

● Galvanized metal containers suit a hi-tech interior.

● For that seaside look, wooden containers can be given a wash of white paint for a weathered, salted appearance.

COOKING WITH HERBS

Most dishes are best with only one or two herbs. Some are very strong and in excess can easily overpower more delicate flavours.

● Pesto is traditionally made by crushing together basil, garlic, and pine nuts and adding olive oil and a hard cheese such as parmesan. However, you can substitute other herbs such as rosemary, parsley, or oregano, using almonds or walnuts in place of the pine nuts.

● Rocket has slightly bitter leaves that make an excellent, palate-cleansing salad, either on their own or with lettuce.

● Bay leaves are delicious in any nursery milk pudding as well as in winter stews and casseroles.

● Basil, the typical Mediterranean herb, is actually from India, so is essential in any Fusion dish.

Right An old metal colander used as an improvised container planted with a mixture of herbs – variegated thyme, basil, and marjoram – provides effective drainage, as well as having that pre-war, granny's kitchen look. The meat tray underneath protects the work surface from water damage, but should be emptied promptly, as most herbs hate sitting with their feet in excess water.

Easy to grow herbs
Chives *Allium schoenoprasum*
Chamomile *Chamaemelum nobile*
Rocket *Eruca vesicaria*
Bay *Laurus nobilis*
Mint *Mentha*
Basil *Ocimum basilicum*
Marjoram *Origanum*
Parsley *Petroselinum crispum*
Rosemary *Rosmarinus officinalis*
Thyme *Thymus* species

CENTREPIECES FOR
THE DINING ROOM

A floral centrepiece is the one essential element of setting the dining table for a special occasion. Without it, the table looks unfinished.

Before choosing a plant for the table, there are several aspects to consider. The first is that the plant should not be more than 25cm (10in) high to make sure that guests can see whoever is seated on the other side. Secondly, avoid plants with too strong a fragrance as this may detract from the aroma of the various dishes served.

STYLING IDEAS

If you decide to create a lunch or dinner party with a theme, then all accessories must carry that theme through, and that includes the style of plant.

● For an oriental theme, choose small, rectangular containers in red or black with a lacquer finish, and fill with single plants such as coral moss (*Nertera granadensis*), which sprouts a dense green mat dotted with bright orange berries. Or consider the bright green mass of mind-your-own-business (*Soleirolia soleirolii*), whose tiny mass of foliage grows to just 5cm (2in).

● Salsa food cries out for cacti. Try a row of fish-hook cacti (*Ferocatus latispinus*) – at 25cm (10in) high, they just meet the height requirements – with aggressive spikes all over their round form. Also, tiger jaws (*Faucaria tigrina*), whose succulent leaves have sharp, jagged edges; it bursts into yellow flowers in autumn.

● Formal occasions require restrained, elegant plants. Slender club-rush (*Isolepsis cernua*) will be perfect all in a row, preferably in glazed white pots.

TABLE DECORATION

Putting a plant in a container and placing it on the table require thought. Most people have a certain dinner service for the occasion. Match the flowers and their pots with the shape and colours in the dinner set and table napkins. Plain services are best. Heavily patterned ones detract from the effect of the plants.

● A white theme: add one or two fashionable platters under a white container, as shown in the photograph left. Think small. For four guests, use four individual plants and platters so they can take them home.

● Create a trailing effect: choose a trailing ivy with variegated green and silvery leaves and place one at each end of the table. Trail the ivy to the centre of the table, where sit three small round candles wrapped in wide silver mesh ribbon. Weave the ivy in and around the ribbon.

● Individual miniature cream roses in rustic pots or baskets placed at each setting, tied with natural fibre bows, create a country-style ambience.

● Several small grape hyacinths (*Muscari armeniacum*) placed evenly along the table can be linked with a trail of ribbon decorated with bunches of grapes.

● Almost translucent, eerie moonstones (*Pachyphytum oviferum*) take table design out of the box and into the future. Place in small, shiny metal containers and put three close together on silver lacquered boxes at either end of the table.

Left Cyclamen are among the best flowering houseplants, with their elegant flowers and exquisitely marked foliage. Here, a variety in virginal white has been matched to a simple glazed pot set on two matching square plates of different sizes. The quiet distinction of this arrangement ceates an interesting focal point, yet will not distract attention from your delicious cooking.

SENSUAL IDEAS FOR
BEDROOMS

We spend up to a third of our lives in bed, which makes it imperative that we pay attention to the plants we place in the rest zone.

Plants in the bedroom help to create a sense of harmony, or excite, depending upon the desired ambience. The sensuality inherent in the form of a dendrobium orchid is breathtaking. These plants lend an exotic air, and many varieties are exquisitely scented. There are thousands of varieties and hybrids to choose from – look for the spare, sensual varieties such as 'Golden Shower'. The latter are best for "learners" since they respond well to watering and feeding. Slipper orchids (*Paphiopedilum*) feature slipper-like flowers – a witty idea for a bedroom – which are produced over an eight-week period between autumn and spring. All orchids need good light, but avoid direct sunlight. A place by the window is best, especially in winter. Artificial lighting enhances flowering, so you may like to investigate the correct type to use.

Scent can overpower in a bedroom, so if you want a fragrant plant choose with care. Consider a delicately scented plant like lavender, which is renowned for its relaxing qualities. A small pot placed on a bedside table is beneficial. There are many varieties to choose from, but all will have the desired effect. It is best to avoid very heavily scented plants such as gardenias and jasmine. On a hot sultry night, the scent could well be too much.

Pelargoniums and primroses are also good choices for the bedroom – they have a wide colour range, so a harmonious look is easy to achieve. For serenity, avoid cluttering surfaces with lots of small pots. One fine flower can leave a memorable impression – bear in mind that less is more, and that the most pleasure is derived from a light touch.

Coloured containers can influence the mood; go for white, cream, pale blue, and soft lilac for serenity. Matt finishes, rather than gloss, are preferable for creating a calm mood.

STYLING IDEAS

Many plants will be at home in a bedroom and can be used to enhance any style you may wish to create.

● For a colonial feel, try a palm such as the majesty palm (*Ravenea rivularis*) in a basket in a corner of the room. A moquito net over the bed and an overhead fan to agitate the air would complete the tropical look.

● A collection of miniature kalanchoes in warm shades of yellow, pink, orange, and red on a bedside table will really glow when lit by a discreet table lamp with a heavy shade.

● A single amaryllis (*Hippeastrum*) on your dressing table can help cheer up those dull winter mornings.

● Choose white moth orchids (*Phalaenopsis*) to go with your pristine, freshly starched Egyptian cotton sheets.

● Place feathery plants near the window to filter the early morning sun, ensuring the gentlest awakening.

Right This dendrobium is just one of many orchids that are suitable for growing in bedrooms. The elegant, arching, cane-like stems nod serenely, complementing the quiet elegance.

PRACTICAL PLANTS FOR
BATHROOMS

Modern bathrooms are sanctuaries from stress; more a personal spa than a basic, functional space for a bath. Here, style is as important as in the rest of the house.

Bathroom fittings are now streamlined to encourage pampering and recuperation. The therapeutic soak can be undertaken in a sensual jet spa bath, or under a power shower generating masses of steam vapour. This steamy environment is the best location for plants that like moisture and humidity.

STYLING IDEAS

Choose one spectacular plant for impact. Something that says in one glance: I am beautiful. This will also reduce clutter: an important consideration in view of the small size of many bathrooms. The rose grape (*Medinilla magnifica*) is perfect. Lush, boldy veined leaves part to display nodding flowers through spring and summer. It is fond of warmth and high humidity but dislikes a draught. This dramatic plant cries out for a similarly exotic container, so look around for a large glazed pot that blends with any other glossy ceramic surface in the bathroom – vivid blue, Chinese red, or shimmering turquoise.

- For a touch of brilliant red look at the flamingo flower (*Anthurium scherzerianium*) and the oilcloth flower (*Anthurium andreanum*). Both are difficult to grow (they need staking), but worth it. The exotic, waxy flowers, with their cheeky curling orange tails, last about two months in spring and summer. They will love the mist.
- Best of all is the gleaming bird's-nest fern (*Asplenium nidus*), which sprouts clumps of bold, long green fronds

from a fibrous, nest-like base. It is a magnificently showy plant and deserves to be seen in a good sized, glossy ceramic container.

- A low-growing, attractive mossy plant that enjoys damp conditions is club moss (*Selaginella*). A shallow pot, filled with well-drained compost, is the ideal way to grow these little beauties. Black and glossy or brash and metallic will make a stylish contrast to the supergreen mass of mossy texture. They dislike direct sun and dry heat, so keep off window ledges and away from radiators.

PLANTING IDEAS

It is important to choose containers that will withstand the damp, steamy atmosphere of a bathroom. Glazed ceramic and most plastic pots are ideal. Those made of cane, bamboo, or wicker will soon show signs of distress unless given a coat of a plant-friendly varnish to protect them from excess moisture.

- African violets (*Saintpaulia*) simply revel in damp conditions. To give them the high humidity they need, try planting them at the base of a large clear glass jar.
- Nearly all the ferns are forest dwellers that actually prefer a damp, steamy environment.
- Try fixing containers of rainforest plants, such as the Christmas cactus (*Schlumbergera*), to the walls of the bathroom to mimic the way they grow in the wild – on trees, well above ground level.

Left The sultry-looking rose grape is an exotic choice for a bathroom. Siting it above the bath, as here, allows you to admire the heavily veined undersides of its leaves and its hanging flowers. It provides a perfect focal point for contemplation whenever you have a relaxing soak.

Steam-loving plants
Bird's nest fern *Asplenium nidus*
Hard fern *Blechnum*
Umbrella grass *Cyperus involucratus*
Boston fern *Nephrolepis exaltata 'Bostoniensis'*
African violet *Saintpaulia*
Christmas cactus *Schlumbergera*

HEALTHY HOME OFFICES

An increasing number of people are opting to work at home, which opens up a new way of looking at the benefits of houseplants in the home/work arena.

Houseplants are beneficial to the atmosphere: they absorb carbon dioxide from the air and replace it with oxygen via photosynthesis; they act as natural ionizers, helping to eradicate harmful toxins and pollutants from the air (including formaldehyde, found in indoor air) and emissions from computers. *Clivia miniata* – a colourful South African perennial, its flower set apart amidst long and broad dark green leaves – is ideal for a solo feature plant on top of a filing cabinet and is decorative even when out of flower.

PLANT PLACEMENT

Working in a restricted area leaves little space for plants. Here's where the century plant (*Agave americana*) and echeverias are useful. Even small plants can act as space dividers, as shown right. Bushy plants are also useful as room dividers, providing an important psychological barrier between work and play zones, especially if your home office occupies a corner of the living area. When relaxing in the evening, they will help you forget it is there.

Tall, leafy species will hide the desktop computer and files. The weeping fig (*Ficus benjamina*) – one of the most tolerant of all indoor plants – is the best low-maintenance option for this situation. It can reach a good height indoors, and will take up a lot of space when mature. The variegated form 'Variegata' has cream-edged leaves, so you could place it between two of the regular variety for greater effect. Choose a large container, and water when the soil feels dry. Feed once a fortnight and watch it grow. Try not to overwater it, since the leaves will then fall off. Don't despair – new ones will replace them. Keep an eye on the leaves for scale insects. If you find them, wash the bugs off the underside of individual leaves with soapy water – tiresome hand-work, but it is effective.

Think carefully where you put smaller containers, since any water spillage could damage computer or other essential equipment, besides posing the risk of electric shock.

BENEFICIAL IONIZERS

All plants will improve the work environment, but particularly good ionizing plants include:
* Boston fern (*Nephrolepsis exaltata* 'Bostoniensis'), producing a permanent show of soft green fronds.
* Peace lily (*Spathiphyllum wallisii* or *S.* 'Mauna Loa'), with the advantage of white, sail-like flowers of breathtaking purity in spring and summer.
* Tulips (*Tulipa*), hardy bulbs that should be grown in containers outdoors and brought inside for enjoyment just as the flowers are starting to open. Short, sturdy varieties are the best for indoor display. After flowering, they can be planted in the garden.

Right Besides their classic good looks, this agave and trio of echeverias are actually good for your health, absorbing and neutralizing harmful pollutants present in the atmosphere.

Ionizing plants
Maidenhair fern *Adiantum raddianum*
Urn plant *Aechmea fasciata*
Jade plant *Crassula ovata*
Ctenanthe 'Golden Mosaic'
Dumb cane *Dieffenbachia seguine*
Peace lily *Spathiphyllum wallisii*

IDEAS FOR
DISPLAYING PLANTS

Having invested in a stunning plant, you will want to make the most of it; deciding where to place it and how best to display it requires careful consideration.

Left One strong plant and pot can stand alone if they are a special match – here, the dramatic and splashy leaves of the begonia (a rex-cultorum type) cleverly echo the bold pattern of this 1960s ceramic planter.

More often than not, plants are displayed on their own on a coffee table, a kitchen bench, or a windowsill. Larger plants are in all likelihood put on the floor in a corner of the room, where they can all too easily fail to make the statement they should.

With a bit of imagination, plants can be star performers, displaying their beauty in a myriad of positions and under a variety of light conditions. Plants are not just for daytime (see pages 116–17). You must treat the plants you chose as if they are pieces of precious antique china or works of art on display in a gallery.

First, you must set the stage. Look around the room and see which surfaces would suit a tableau of your favourite plants. Piles of illustrated books and decorative ceramic fruit bowls would complement a wide-lipped container planted with a luxurious pink orchid, for example. Create this look on top of a lacquered console table used to divide a seating area from the rest of the room. You can move this around at any time to alter the ambience of the room.

In hip homes with modern furnishings, go for cool expanses of flooring or shelving, broken up with shots of colour provided by foliage or flowering plants. For a dynamic look, display the plants at different levels on modern steel and glass, iron, or timber shelving units –

moving from left to right, beginning with the top, middle, and then the lower section.

Alternatively, look for a display unit that is in keeping with the style of your room, with individual spaces in which to display exotic plants. Each will be quite at home in its own niche. Place the unit against an expanse of plain wall to make the greatest impact, or use it as a room divider, so you can view the plants from both sides.

Unusual furniture such as a French-style delicate wrought-iron table found in an antique market or a slab of marble on top of a timber table make original display surfaces; or place a hand-made ceramic tile, a memento from a holiday abroad, under the plant.

You can also place plants one under the other on a plant stand, as people did in the 19th century; only update the look by choosing a more modern plant stand (or make one, if you are so inclined) and up-to-the-minute plants. Position flowering plants on top, bushy or trailing plants in the middle, and a compact but colourful plant in the lowest compartment. Place in a corner of a room with reasonable light. Alternatively, you can allow your most treasured plant to take pride of place on the coffee table in the middle of the room, but take care to avoid splashes on the surface when watering.

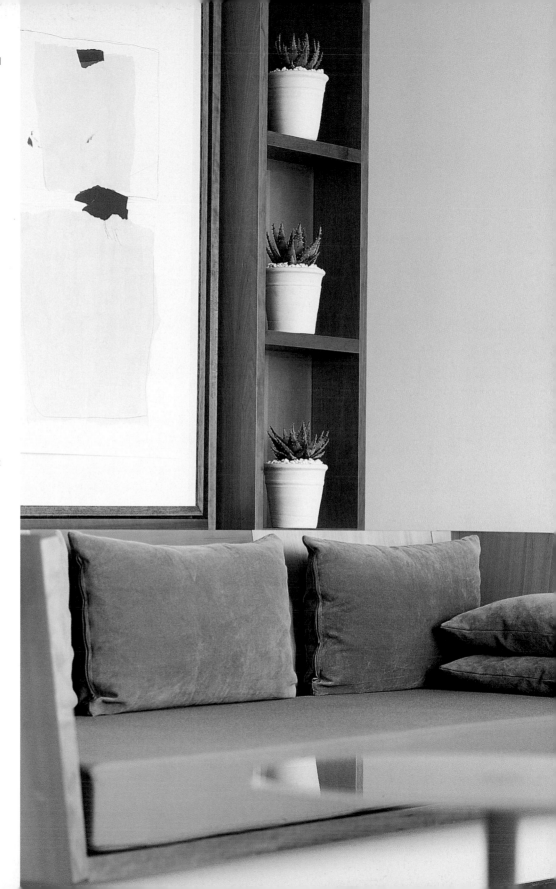

Top far left The individual boxes on this shelving unit frame a collection of cacti. Although each cactus is an individual, there is a harmony to the arrangement as a trio of different pots and plants are repeated.

Top left Ferns soften the geometric lines of this coffee table.

Bottom far left Corkscrew rushes, in pots that echo the plant's curls in their ridges, are lined up along a table centre.

Bottom left One spectacular aloe takes pride of place on this console table.

Right The power of three: identical plants make more of an impact than a selection would.

Left Pretty pansies in a charming trough bring summer indoors.

Top right Shells are used to cover the compost in the pots and also as decorative trim along the edges of the baskets.

Bottom right An antique wrought-iron gate has been made into a plant stand that holds several pots. Look for purpose-designed stands of your chosen period in markets and antique shops.

POTS

CONTAINERS

CHOOSING CONTAINERS

A container is to a plant what a shoe is to a human – it must be able to slip into it comfortably, have extra room for growth, and be of the right style, naturally.

There is such a wealth of variety in containers nowadays that it is easy to link them with the style of the interior. Choose carefully – the shape and size should be in direct proportion to the fully grown plant.

MATERIALS

- Cutting-edge concrete pots may need a hole drilling in the bottom to allow for good drainage. Being unglazed, they are not waterproof. They look good for a while but need looking after.
- Terracotta pots, now available in a wide range of styles and sizes (from tiny to enormous), are porous, and plants potted in them will need regular watering. Soak terracotta pots in water overnight before using.
- Plastic pots retain water and plants will not need watering so frequently. They are often moulded to imitate natural materials such as terracotta, stone, or lead, and are generally considerably cheaper than the genuine article.
- Tin and metal pots can rust, so check that they have a protective finish when you buy them. When using old iron and metal containers, put the plant in a plain plastic pot and slip that inside.
- Bamboo containers are chic but not that practical, since they tend to split after a while. Slip a plastic pot inside, if necessary, to protect the material against water damage.
- Consider a wooden outer container if you live in a modern space with wooden floors.

- Glass containers look sleek and sophisticated and allow you to monitor plant roots. Careful potting can produce a two-tone effect of compost and drainage material.

DRAINAGE

This is ultimately the step that will determine whether you will kill a plant quickly or set it on the road to a healthy life. To enable a plant to drain effectively, line the bottom of your container with small pieces of clay from a broken garden pot, or stones, pebbles, or even polystyrene pieces; this provides a base for the potting medium and the plant's roots. Make sure that this layer is about 5cm (2in) deep. Put the potting mixture on top and then add the plant, pushing down the potting mix as you go. The drainage layer lets the water seep through more quickly than if there were just compost on the bottom of the container, which tends to retain moisture. Adding grit to the compost further improves drainage.

- If using a see-through container, be artistic with the drainage layer; turn the container around every now and then to check that the material is even. Empty the container out and repot, if necessary.
- If a pot does not have a hole in the bottom, use a deeper layer of drainage material and add charcoal to the compost to keep it sweet.
- If the container is not waterproof line with plastic sheeting; if the pot has drainage holes stand in a saucer.

Right Pure white hand-made pots in unglazed earthenware. Visit small potteries or craft fairs for one-off designs.

Top far left Chunkily rustic, these hand-made pots are nevertheless supremely practical.

Top left These glazed white pots have a sleek, retro 1950s feel and suit any minimalist interior.

Bottom far left The slippery, glazed insides of these coloured pots are actually very beneficial to any plants that need swift drainage.

Bottom left Factory-made terracotta pots are always a reliable choice. Look for slightly taller shapes for a modern feel.

Right Giving pots an initial wash with a water-based paint is a quick way of giving them that bespoke look.

Left The texture of this silvery-leaved Mexican hat plant perfectly echoes that of the dark concrete container that it is about to be potted into.

Top right Dyed concrete pots are the perfect complement to these campanulas. A top-dressing of white chippings completes the industrial look.

Bottom right Here, the glossy, hand-shaped leaves of a tree ivy contrast strongly with the containers.

Far left A craftsman-made stone pot such as this one is a real one-off. Look out for them at craft shows and galleries or commission one to your own specifications.

Top left Consider the pot's texture: shiny; matt; or strongly patterned. Demand plants that will stand up to their dramatic looks.

Bottom left Hand-made pots can be relied on to add a note of distinction to any setting.

Bottom far left Look out for industrial containers – old or new. These galvanized steel boxes make an original choice for a planter.

Bottom left Aluminium and tin containers do not rust but often acquire an attractive patina with age. They make an excellent foil to many houseplants.

Bottom right These terracotta pots have been sprayed silver. Top-dressing the compost with stone chippings gives a contemporary finish.

Bottom far right Galvanized and enamelled buckets can make superb containers. Put a layer of stone chippings in the bottom to aid drainage.

Top far left Lime-washed cylindrical wooden pots look like sections of tree-trunk, and are ideal for any collection of African plants.

Top left The textured surface of these balsa wood pots complements the plants' dense mop of leaves.

Bottom far left These smooth, shiny pots are actually made of coconut wood that has been varnished to produce a glassy finish.

Bottom left Teak and mahogany are heavy and substantial materials for plant pots, if expensive. They are strong decorative objects in their own right.

Right Bowls made of bamboo are inexpensive, lightweight, and fresh-looking – making them an ideal way to bring a contemporary note to houseplant collections.

Left These tall, narrow, matt-glazed pots in contrasting cream and black are a sophisticated and modern choice for a wide range of plants.

Top right Rubber and its synthetic equivalents have not been widely used for houseplants, but the modern trend is increasingly to explore the possibilities of such unusual materials.

Bottom right Here, a matt black pot stands on a pair of plinths to show off the elegant, arching lines of the fern.

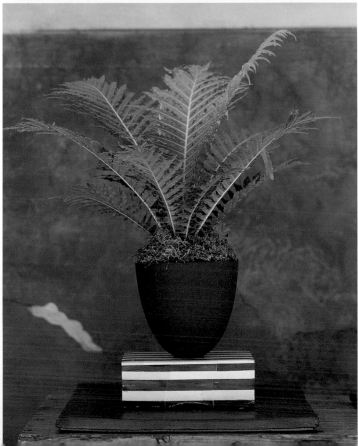

IMPROVISING
CONTAINERS

Enhance the display of your houseplants by creating original containers from household objects. Transform basic pots with paint, pebbles, moss, or shells.

Containers are important when linking plants to the style of the surroundings, and you can always change them to suit your mood. I like to compare the container or cachepot (an ornamental container for a flowerpot) that houses a plant to the perfect pair of shoes or the essential fashion accessory that round off an outfit.

Often, a simple effect will add drama to an otherwise mundane container – and you don't have to break the bank to achieve impressive results. For example, you could salvage an old colander and use it to plant a practical herb display in the kitchen (see pages 72–73).

Customizing containers can be great fun and need not be intimidating. I am not a great fan of the plain, standard factory-produced terracotta pots which, although inexpensive, lack the character of the hand-thrown versions. However, they are the perfect candidates for customizing, as they are designed for holding plants and are readily available in varying sizes from most shops and garden centres.

Terracotta pots can be painted or sprayed in strong, bold colours for modern environments (see pages 14–15), pastel shades for a more calm and muted setting such as a bedroom, or metallic colours like gold or silver to add a festive note. The results can be enhanced by applying a PVA (polyvinyl acetate) coating which dries to a clear finish and gives the pot a professional look as well as a waterproof covering.

STYLING IDEAS

Provided you consider the drainage aspect and ensure that it is waterproof, don't rule out anything that has the depth or shape to accommodate a plant.

● Transparent vases offer interesting opportunities for transformation. I use a variety of materials, including white stones, pebbles, or shells between the plastic pot and the vase to hide the pot (see right).

● Basic plastic pots can be surrounded by twigs, covered with leaves, or camouflaged with moss.

● I have discovered that leather or woven rattan boxes – often used for the domestic storage of clothing – make wonderful and unusual containers for plants. To make a box waterproof, line it with a piece of heavy-duty plastic covered with a thin layer of gravel to keep it in place.

The improvised containers featured on the opposite page have been conceived around a beachcombing theme. Have fun thinking of themes to suit your home – for example, an industrial look can be achieved by using rows of matching empty food cans stripped of their labels (see pages 72–73).

Top right The addition of twigs and shells "softens" these galvanized containers and gives them a more natural look.

Top far right A glass vase is brought to life by the addition of miniature shells that also camouflage the plastic pot inside.

Bottom right This container was originally a fishing basket. The wire mesh and stones enhance the appeal of this succulent echeveria.

Bottom far right The beading on the edge of the plain basket chimes with the shell trim used to cover the potting compost.

PAINTING POTS

For a unique container, try your hand at painting an ordinary clay pot. Any craft store stocks a wide range of paints and brushes suitable for this endeavour. Most people want to decorate pots in order to produce an individual container in a colour or colours that are in harmony with their interior design scheme.

● Decide which style and colours are best by analysing design features in the room. Which colour is dominant? Is there a definite shape and form visible in the furnishings – for instance, does the furniture feature curves or straight lines? You may like to echo the dominant lines in a design on the container.

● Figure painting requires a steady hand. You may prefer to copy a shape onto tracing paper, then transfer the shape to the pot in pencil and, finally, colour it in. Keep the shape simple and you will be successful.

● Stripes are easy to paint. Work out the colour scheme first on a piece of paper. Place the bare pot on a sheet of newspaper on a worktop and sit down in front of it. If you don't feel very confident, draw pencil lines of where each colour is to go around the pot first. Hold the loaded paint brush against the surface of the pot with one hand, and, with the other, rotate the pot at the speed you feel most comfortable with.

Bottom far left Apply a base colour of blue and, when dry, stick on tissue paper shapes with PVA. Allow these to dry, then glue on the patches of gold leaf. Once the glue has dried, varnish with a coating of PVA.

Bottom left For this Matisse-inspired pot, first apply two or three base coats of white emulsion. Draw the figures onto blue paper, cut them out, and stick them on with PVA. Apply a couple of coats of PVA to finish the pot.

Bottom right These random stripes on an unglazed terracotta pot are created with acrylic paints. To prevent the colours from running into each other, allow each stripe to dry before adding the next.

Bottom far right Marc Chagall, eat your heart out! First paint on an undercoat of white emulsion. Outline the shapes with black oil pastel, then fill in using oil paints and oil pastels (do not mix the two). Finish with an oil-based varnish.

USING
SURFACE TRIMS

The big cover-up of unsightly compost has become a fashion trend and is one to be considered seriously for the added decorative impact it gives.

Regardless of the size and shape of the container, mounds of compost always creep over the rim and lie there, on the tabletop. Adding surface trims is one way of keeping pot plants tidy and it adds an extra decorative element, giving you more opportunities to create a stylish planting. However, its real importance is in the practical benefits it brings by preserving moisture in the potting mixture, and helping to keep it warm. It also helps keep the collars of plants dry.

MATERIALS

In recent years, a fantastic array of surface trims has become available through florists' suppliers and specialist stores. As with the containers, the choice of a trim is dictated by the style and growth habit of the plant, as well as the look you are aiming to create.

● Shards of smooth slate provide an option for plants with sturdy stems and foliage that begins a little way up the stems. Look for thin, level slivers that will sit evenly on top of the compost.

● Round black or dark brown pebbles are great with larger, brightly coloured plants, providing an attractive contrast. Look for smooth pebbles that fit snugly in the palm of your hand. Coated with a plant-friendly gloss varnish, they will appear permanently wet.

● Traditional moss is still a favourite of many indoor gardeners. It sits happily on top of the soil, bouncing up

and out of the rim – but in a refined way. Take care not to let it get too dry. Misting occasionally will help keep it fresh and alive.

● Shells from the beach will add a seaside air to a pot, particularly one that's a watery pale or dark blue.

● Opalescent pebbles are best for fragile plants, echoing perhaps their creamy blooms or pale variegated foliage.

● Bark is fabulous under dark foliage plants. It can be a mix of sizes and shapes, but check that it doesn't harbour any pests and is free from signs of mould before adding it to the container.

● Small chips of white, crystal-like stones look cool with cacti, especially in a room with a monochromatic scheme. They suit high-tech metal or highly glazed pots rather well.

● Glass discs take on a new dimension when used as a surface trim for many plants. In a glass or acrylic container they can add colour as well as helping to sustain the illusion of transparency.

When adding trim, do not overfill the container or press the trim down too hard on top of the compost. You must allow the compost to breathe and not put pressure on the roots.

Remember that as fashion colours change in both plants and containers, so you can mix and match the trim. Don't throw away old ones, since you never know what your mood will dictate.

Top right Fine gravel, small stones, and smashed shells.

Top far right Sphagnum moss is available bagged up at florists and garden centres. Immerse it in water for a while before use, and spray it occasionally to keep it green and fresh.

Bottom right Glass pebbles, both polished and unpolished, are available in a range of jewel-like colours.

Bottom far right Polished stones are wonderful just to hold and look at, aside from their practical value as trims.

LIGHTING

NATURAL DAYLIGHT

Plants definitely thrive in natural daylight, growing automatically towards it from wherever they are located in a room.

Plants require light to carry out photosynthesis, which in turn allows them to live a long and healthy life. Certain exotic plants thrive in full sunlight more than others, although not necessarily in direct sunlight, as this can singe the foliage and their delicate blooms. Light enhances flowers; it filters through their colourful petals, creating pale light patterns on surfaces around them. You can almost feel them unfold and revel in the warmth, so if you have a window with a sill deep enough for an extravagant plant that's a perfect focal point, do not hesitate to put it there. If direct sun shines on the window even for ten minutes a day, you should shade the plant with a blind that lets in light but filters the rays.

Take note of where and when the daylight is brightest in the room and place the plants that love those conditions there. A room is darker the closer to the ceiling, so when hanging baskets or placing plants on top of display cabinets and bookshelves, check their growing preferences. Many ivy varieties (*Hedera*) and that wonderful classic plant the leafy aspidistra (*Aspidistra elatior*) are usually happy in this environment.

Moderate light is ideal for most houseplants, which means a spot near a window, but not in strong sunny conditions. If a plant has not been performing well, move it closer to the window and you will soon see it perk up.

In the kitchen, a sunny windowsill is ideal for growing herbs such as basil, sage, and lemon-scented thyme. Keep an eye on the watering regime. Other sunny windowsill plants include cacti, bougainvillea (you can train them to grow in a compact way), and rose geraniums (*Pelargonium* 'Graveolens').

BULBS – GROWING TIPS

Bulbs are storage organs that allow the plant to survive adverse weather conditions by becoming dormant below ground. Amaryllises (*Hippeastrum* hybrids), zantedeschias, and freesias can be grown indoors. Tulips, hyacinths, narcissi, crocuses, and daffodils are actually garden bulbs but can also be grown indoors. Growing bulbs indoors "forces" them to flower well ahead of those in the garden.

- To ensure flowering, buy bulbs from a supplier with a reliable reputation.
- Plant bulbs in August through to October for flowers in January to April.
- For Christmas-flowering hyacinths, plant bulbs in September (northern hemisphere).
- Keep bowls and containers in the dark in a cold place during the root development period, then provide heat and light to promote growth of leaves and flowers.
- Prefer tulips with strong stems, and provide some form of support as they grow.

Right Amaryllises and hyacinths are ideal bulbs for a sunny windowsill. Make sure that you rotate the plants regularly so that the stems grow upright – they tend to lean towards the sun. Tall varieties can be top-heavy, and often benefit from staking with a cane or length of thin bamboo.

Other plants for full daylight
Agave victoriae-reginae
Aloe
Paper flower *Bougainvillea*
Desert cacti
Citrus
Echeveria
Euphorbia abyssinica
Olive *Olea europea*

DRAMATIC
HALOGEN

Since the advent of the halogen bulb, lighting has brought a new dimension to the concept of spotlighting specific houseplants.

Top left This reading lamp, focussed on a spiky dracaena, lights up the dramatic variegation of its leaves.

Top far left Halogen lamps specifically designed for houseplants can be plunged in the compost surface to create moody shadows on the walls and ceiling.

Bottom left Don't save fairy lights just for the Christmas tree! Here, they create a soft, glamorous, Hollywood chic.

Bottom far left The feathery shadows cast by this kentia palm seem to double the plant's size.

Plants for artificial light
Bird's nest fern *Asplenium nidus*
Cast-iron plant *Aspidistra elatior*
Dendrobium hybrids
Tree ivy *Fatshedera lizei*
Moth orchid *Phalaenopsis* hybrids

Lighting in a domestic situation plays an important role in creating atmosphere, be it during the day or at night. It is a subsititute for, as well as an addition to, natural daylight. Halogen fixtures emit a clear white light that is almost like daylight. Clever use creates subtle interplays of light and shade to soften and enhance the decoration of a room. Directional light – the sort provided by a spotlight – picks out the detail, and in the case of houseplants it can really make the foliage come to life and the beauty in the flowers shine through. When directional light is played upon a kentia palm the shadow effects are cast against the wall, revealing the wonderful form of its foliage. It is also useful for highlighting the unique characteristics of a plant such as an amaryllis or exotic bromeliad. Always check if the plant can stand lighting effects. Some foliage is too fragile for the heat that a light bulb of any kind generates, and halogens generate quite a lot.

TYPES OF ARTIFICIAL LIGHT

There are three popular categories:
● Tungsten, the most common form of domestic lighting: a warm light that makes oranges and red seem brighter and blues seem dull.
● Tungsten halogen: a white light that makes blues less dull, and adds a sparkling vitality to a room. Fittings operate on mains voltage and low voltage (usually with a small transformer), and both can be dimmed. Most commonly seen in desklamps and spotlights is the smaller-size halogen reflector bulb.
● Fluorescent: once considerd a harsh light, recent developments have made this more user-friendly.

DESIGNING WITH LIGHT

Depending on the fitting, light can be distributed evenly in all directions, in one direction, in a concentrated ray. Lighting designers use lights in four different ways: as background lighting, uplighting, task lighting, and accent lighting.
● Background lighting provides a general replacement for daylight and usually comes from a ceiling light (pendant or fitted). The alternatives are wall brackets, free-standing uplights, and table lamps.
● Task lighting is used at kitchen benches and desks in home offices to illuminate work surfaces.
● Accent lighting is mainly used to highlight displays and create a sense of theatre. This type is suitable for most houseplants.

Spotlights are usually fitted to the ceiling, beaming a pool of light down, but you can fit them to the wall. Some designs clip to a shelf so they can be moved around. These are also good for lighting plants. Or a track with several lights can be fitted to a ceiling and the spots can move along to highlight individual plants.

CREATIVE
ILLUMINATION

Plants can put on a show-stopping display, and it makes perfect sense to illuminate them in an imaginative and intelligent way.

Informal lighting provided by candles is an acceptable alternative method to electric lighting that allows you to create different moods every time. It's a more fun, relaxed way of illuminating an exciting group of plants. Used imaginatively, the results can be impressive.

Candles are big business and come in a wide range of sizes and colours. Use the same decorating rules that you apply to choosing a plant: does the candle colour match or harmonize with the basic colour theme? Is the size right – not too overwhelming or too tiny to make an impact? For a romantic mood, choose cream or red (if using potted roses, for instance), and, for party times, use ritzier purples, blues, golds, and silvers.

IDEAS FOR CANDLES

● Make a circle of flames around two or three small pot plants. Choose candles which are lower than the height of the pots.

● Place small, square candles at each corner of a rectangular container, with the height of the candles level with the height of the container.

● Two tall candleholders set in the midst of a group of shorter containers filled with colourful flowers and foliage will enhance the beauty of the grouping.

● Tea lights placed in the bottom of small pots will cast a

soft light over plants. Use them imaginatively (see opposite) – one candle, then one plant placed in a neat row. The plant must have compact growth, as does the mind-your-own-business (*Soleirolia soleirolii*).

● For a special event, hang light containers on fine wire next to colourful Chinese lanterns in a location where no one will walk into them (see right).

● Try balancing tiny pots on a large, solid candelabrum. Fix the pots with adhesive, one at each far side, then place a candle in the next branch, on each side, and so on until you reach the top, where you can fix the star plant.

CANDLE SAFETY

Of course, you have to take on board the safety issues involved in using fire. A naked flame can easily singe plant leaves, so take care not to place the candle too close to the plant. Also, do not use a candle in a situation where paper, fabric, or any other flammable material could easily catch fire, and make sure there is someone in the room at all times when the candle is lit.

CANDLE ALTERNATIVES

For a festive occasion, take liberties with tiny Christmas tree lights. You can hang, wrap, and drape them in and around the leaves of tough plants, if it is for a short time only, or around the container.

Top right Schlumbergeras in bud actually look like candles, an impression enhanced by the shallow tray of short candles at their feet.

Top far right A Chinese paper lantern casts a subtle glow.

Bottom right Christmas tree lights have ensnared this phallic-looking guzmania in flower.

Bottom far right A chorus-line of mind-your-own-business alternating with candles in matching ceramic pots.

PLANT CARE

UNDERSTANDING
SOIL HEALTH

The soil, or potting compost, is one of the greatest influences on the health and well-being of your plants. It is important to choose the right type and to keep it in good order.

Always buy a good-quality compost; cheap ones of dubious origins may contain weed seed or even pests and diseases. They are often old stock in which the fertilizer has broken down and is no longer effective. Garden soil is unsuitable for houseplants. It can also harbour weed seed as well as insect pests and diseases. Within the confines of a pot, soil bacteria can build up to levels that are toxic to plants. Proprietary composts have exactly the right balance of plant nutrients, as well as a loose, light texture.

TYPES OF COMPOST

There are several types of compost. In the first place there is the option of either soil-less or soil-based types. There are advocates for both. In the end, the choice comes down to which you find easiest to use. Some people find they get better results with one rather than the other, while others find it easier to work, particularly with regard to watering, with one particular brand.

● Soil-based composts are heavy to carry home but the weight helps to prevent the pots being accidentally knocked over. They are easier to re-water than soil-less ones, should you allow them to dry out.

● Soil-less composts are lighter to carry but the pots, especially with tall plants in them, can easily fall over if the compost dries out. These composts can be very difficult to water once they have dried out. (Try adding a spot of washing-up liquid to the water, should this occur.)

● Fertilizer: soil-less composts rely entirely on the added fertilizers for their nutrients, whereas the soil-based ones contain a certain amount of nutrient in the loam as well as having some added fertilizers.

● Many soil-less varieties are still based on peat – the use of which many gardeners feel is environmentally unacceptable. If this is an issue for you, look for composts based on coir or some other renewable resource.

The second choice to be made is regarding the relevance of the composts. Many plants will cope well with any good potting compost, but others, such as ericaceous plants (azaleas, gardenias, and heathers, for example) or orchids, need a specially formulated compost. Bromeliads and cacti also need special formulas. It is sometimes advisable (if not always strictly necessary) to add grit, perlite, or vermiculite to standard compost to improve drainage. Plants from woodland areas, such as ferns, often appreciate additions of bark chippings to the compost, to simulate the conditions of the forest floor.

Never buy too much compost at any one time. It is not only bulky to store but also it tends to deteriorate on contact with the air, the fertilizer losing its effectiveness. Plan to repot all your plants at the same time and buy just enough compost for the task. After repotting, keep the plants well watered to help them re-establish.

Right Most good-quality proprietary potting composts have a loose, fibrous, crumbly texture and are sweet-smelling.

CAREFUL WATERING

Water is essential to any plant's life – without it, it will die, as it will be unable to manufacture food and carry out other essential activities.

Left All living things need water to survive, and learning how much and how often to water your plants is an essential aspect of keeping them healthy. Check over your plants daily: you will soon arrive at a regime that suits both you and the plants in your collection.

Drought-tolerant plants
Agave
Aloe
Cast-iron plant *Aspidistra elatior*
Desert cacti
Euphorbia abyssinica
Haworthia

Watering is one of the most important aspects of caring for your indoor plants. A bad watering regime is the cause of far more deaths amongst indoor plants than either pests or diseases. Most people use tap water for their plants. Generally this is not a problem, although it is always a good idea to fill a watering can and let it stand for several hours before using it. This will allow any chlorine gas to be given off, as well as ensuring that the water temperature is brought up to that of the room and plant.

The best routine is to refill the can after you have finished watering the plants so that it is ready for your next session. There are a limited number of ericaceous plants, gardenias for example, which do not like alkaline water, which is water containing lime or chalk. In hard water areas there may be sufficient lime in the water to kill the plants. In this situation, it is advisable to collect rainwater (in a plastic water butt) or to use cooled boiled water.

The art of watering is to give the plant just enough. Not enough water and the plant wilts, too much water and the leaves turn yellow and fall off and the plant soon rots. If in doubt, err on the side of less rather than more water. To water from below, stand the plant in a dish of water and allow the soil to suck up the water. This has the advantage of not wetting the leaves or crown of the plant. For soil-less composts that have completely dried out this may be the only method of re-wetting the compost. The other method is to water from above with a watering can. Soak the compost thoroughly and allow excess water to drain away. Do not water again until the compost is almost dry and then wet thoroughly again. Do not water if the compost is already wet. During the dormant season, when a plant is resting, apply only a little water, to keep the soil barely moist. Increase the amount if the plant starts to shrivel.

Some plants (notably orchids, African violets, and other plants that originate in rainforests) appreciate high humidity, and the best way of achieving this is to mist the plants once or twice a day during the growing season (usually spring to summer). Alternatively, stand the pots on trays of wetted clay pellets (available from garden centres) that release moisture around the plant gradually.

There are various aids to make your watering regime easier, including self-watering containers as well as water-retaining granules or crystals that can be added to the compost. Some people find these a great help, others fail to get on with them and prefer to rely on manual watering, over which they feel they have more control. When on holiday, ask a friend to keep an eye on your plants for you. Grouping all the plants together in a spot sheltered from hot sun will raise the humidity around them, and the compost will dry out more slowly.

REGULAR FEEDING

Plants – like humans – need food to keep them alive. As the owner of a houseplant, it is entirely over to you to keep it on the planet.

Most of your houseplants' requirements are manufactured by the plant using water and sunlight, as well as the carbon dioxide in the atmosphere, a process known as photosynthesis. However, there are a number of nutrients that are also essential to its healthy well-being. In the open garden many of these are contained within the soil or added by the application of humus (vegetable remains that break down in the soil). In the indoor garden, they have to be added artificially in the form of fertilizer or plant feed. Although all composts contain some fertilizer in their make-up, much of this is either used up or washed out (leached) by the continual passage of water through the compost from regular irrigation. It is vital to replace this if you want to keep your plants healthy.

There are several ways of doing this. One is to add solid fertilizer to the compost and the second is to provide it in a soluble form added to the water at watering time. Solid fertilizer comes in several different forms. The current favourite is what is known as a slow-release fertilizer. When added to the soil, this takes several months to break down, gently releasing its nutrients over the whole period. This reduces feeding to only once or twice a year. These slow-release fertilizers may come in granules which are mixed into the compost or as a "plug" or a "spike", a cluster of granules that are stuck together, which is inserted whole just below the surface.

An alternative method is to use a liquid feed. This is added to the water in prescribed quantities and applied at regular intervals as stated on the label of the container. A variant to this is a foliar feed, whereby the feed is added to water but it is then sprayed onto the foliage rather than poured with a watering can into the compost. The fertilizer is then absorbed by the plant through its leaves. This is a useful way for prescribing a quick-pick-me-up for an ailing plant, since the nutrients are immediately available.

Most plants are happy with a general or standard fertilizer. Such fertilizers are often described as "balanced": the main plant nutrients, nitrogen, potassium, and phosphorus, are present in equal amounts. There are also specific ones for specific plants. A tomato liquid feed, which is high in potassium, is often a good choice for encouraging flowering plants - particularly orchids – to bloom.

The frequency with which you feed will depend on the type of fertilizer you are using, but details are always given on the packaging. You should only feed a plant when it is producing new leaves. Some products need to be diluted, but some are available ready-mixed, and these are obviously preferable if you are short of time. Do not exceed the recommended dose. Excess fertilizer can be toxic to plants. Plants that are dormant or resting, generally during the winter months, do not require any feed.

Right Fertilizers are magic potions, keeping your houseplants healthy and helping them to perform to their optimum. If you need to dilute the fertilizer, always follow the manufacturer's instructions. Do not store excess feed. You should also not introduce any surplus into the public drainage system: dispose of it by watering it over a path or driveway.

Don't need to feed plants
Castor-oil plant *Aspidistra elatior*
Hard fern *Blechnum*
Spider plant *Chlorophytum comosum* 'Vittatum'
Guzmania lingulata
Hyacinth *Hyacinthus orientalis* hybrids
Hydrangea *Hydrangea macrophylla* hybrids

TIME FOR
REPOTTING

Indoor plants should not be left indefinitely in the same compost – change it for fresh at least once a year to give your plants a new lease of life.

Top far left The roots of this plant have emerged from the base of the pot. Potting on is well overdue.

Top left Slide the plant from the container. If the roots are very congested, as here, it may be necessary to cut off the old pot with scissors.

Bottom far left Prepare the new container by putting a layer of grit, small stones, or pot shards at the base.

Bottom left Holding the plant in the centre of the pot, feed in fresh compost around the sides with your other hand.

For a growing plant this means potting on into a larger pot, but for mature plants that have reached their maximum pot size it means replacing some or all of the compost and returning the plant to the same or a similar-sized pot.

When a young plant is first introduced to a pot this is known as "potting" or "potting up". A seedling, cutting, or division is put into a pot that will just accommodate its root ball. Never place a plant into too large a pot straightaway. Water will collect in the compost not occupied by plant roots, leading to stagnant conditions. Place some drainage material such as pot shards, stones, or gravel in the bottom of the pot to allow free drainage. Put some compost on top of this and then suspend the plant in the centre of the pot with one hand while filling it with compost with the other. Firm it down so that the final level of compost is level with the original planting depth of the young plant. Be sure to leave a gap between the compost surface and the rim of the pot to allow for watering. Press a fertilizer plug into the compost so it sits just below the compost surface and water the pot thoroughly.

As the plant grows, so the roots begin to fill the pot. Never allow this to get to the point where the roots are tightly wound around the inside of the pot. (However, some flowering plants, such as clivias, appreciate being a little pot-bound: the stress seems to make them flower their hearts out.) Just as the roots begin to circle round the sides of the pot (roots will often also show through the drainage holes at this stage), remove the plant from its container and "pot on". Use the next size of container up, first having placed a layer of drainage material in the bottom. Also place a layer of the appropriate compost in the bottom so that the top of the original root ball comes to just below the pot's rim. Fill in the gap around the root ball with fresh compost and water to settle the plant in.

Continue to pot on in this way every year until the plant is in the largest pot or until it has finished growing. At this stage it becomes necessary to "repot" into the same size pot. If possible, remove the plant from the pot and then scrape way as much of the compost as you can without disturbing the roots too much. Repot the plant in the normal way into the same pot or into a new one of the same size. If you are returning the plant to the same pot, scrub it out first with a mild, plant-friendly disinfectant to kill off any bacteria.

If the pot or the plant is too large for you to be able to remove the plant easily, tilt it on its side and scrape away as much of the surface compost as you are able to and then replace this with fresh compost. This process is generally referred to as topdressing.

DEALING WITH
PESTS & DISEASES

Many indoor gardeners become worried about the problems of pests and diseases. Don't fret unduly – just follow the advice below.

Given healthy conditions and good compost there should be few problems caring for houseplants. Having said that, you should be prepared for any problems that might occur.

PREVENTIVE CARE

If you follow this advice the chances of problems will be reduced considerably:

- Check all new plants before bringing them into your home to make sure that they are not themselves carrying pests or diseases.
- Feed and water plants correctly and make sure that the compost is in good condition.
- Keep plants in a light, airy place that is not in a draught or hot sunlight.
- Remove dead leaves and spent flowers immediately, as these can harbour fungi.
- The best defence against both pests and diseases is to make sure that the plants are healthy. Starved, sickly plants are far more susceptible to passing ailments than those that have been looked after.

PESTS

Always check your plants when you water them to make sure that there are no pests lurking among the leaves. If caught at an early stage, most can be picked off with the fingers or a pair of tweezers. Alternatively, wash them off with a spray of soapy water. If the outbreak has become severe before you notice it, the only really satisfactory way of coping with it is to use a relevant chemical spray. Insecticides are changing all the time, so check with your garden centre as to which is best formulated to solve your problem. Do not drench the whole plant but concentrate on the area infested by the insects. Stop as soon as the infestation has been eradicated.

In the open garden, beneficial insects such as ladybirds and lacewings are useful biological controls as they attack pests such as aphids. These are not so useful for houseplants, although they might work in greenhouses and conservatories where there is a wide variety of flowering plants and plenty of open windows. However, if you want to avoid chemicals, there are other forms of biological control which can be used against specific pests, and these can be ordered with advice from garden centres.

DISEASES

Good hygiene, healthy plants, and vigilance, including the removal of any damaged or bruised leaves and stems and dusting the cuts with a fungicide, will reduce the risk of diseases. Regular examination can preempt major outbreaks of a disease, leaving the use of chemicals as almost the last resort. The final solution is to throw the plant away and replace it with a healthy specimen.

Right Ladybirds are beneficial creatures that feed on insect pests. They do not normally find their way indoors, so it is worth opening a few windows occasionally or placing your plants outdoors in good weather to take advantage of these charming do-gooders.

Bad bugs
Whitefly
Aphids
Red spider mites
Scale insects
Mealybugs
Vine weevil

Diseases
Downy mildew
Powdery mildew
Sooty mould
Viruses
Rusts
Leaf spots
Verticillium wilt

PLANT MAINTENANCE

☼ **Light**
🌡 **Temperature**
💧 **Feeding**
💧 **Watering**
▭ **Compost**

Adiantum raddianum *Maidenhair fern*
Height to 60cm (24in), spread 80cm (32in)
These elegant ferns are ideal for growing either on their own or with other houseplants. They appreciate humidity, so make good bathroom plants
☼ Bright indirect light in summer, bright filtered light in winter 🌡 No lower than 7°C (45°F) in winter 💧 Green houseplant fertilizer every 4 weeks in spring and summer 💧 Freely when in growth, sparingly in winter; stand plants on trays of wetted pebbles to increase humidity ▭ Standard fern compost

Aechmea fasciata *Urn plant*
Height to 40cm (16in), spread 50cm (20in)
Urn plants have showy, bright sugar-pink and mauve flowers in summer, but their thick, strap-shaped, silvery grey leaves are attractive throughout the year
☼ Bright filtered light 🌡 No lower than 10°C (50°F) in winter 💧 Flowering houseplant fertilizer every 4 weeks in spring and summer 💧 Keep the central "cup" filled with soft water ▭ Standard bromeliad compost

Aechmea nudicaulis
Height to 70cm (28in), spread 25cm (10in)
These plants have shiny, strap-like leaves and yellow flowers surrounded by showy red bracts in summer
☼ Bright filtered light 🌡 No lower than 10°C (50°F) in winter 💧 Flowering houseplant fertilizer every 4 weeks in spring and summer 💧 Keep the central "cup" filled with soft water ▭ Standard bromeliad compost

Agave victoriae-reginae
Height to 50cm (20in), spread 50cm (20in)
These succulents have thick, spiny leaves. Curving spikes of creamy-white flowers, sometimes tinged purple, appear in summer
☼ Full light 🌡 No lower than 10°C (50°) in winter 💧 Flowering houseplant fertilizer every 4 weeks in spring and summer 💧 Water freely in spring and summer, less in autumn, and sparingly in winter ▭ Standard cactus compost

Alocasia sanderiana *Elephant's ear plant*
Height to 2m (6ft), spread 2m (6ft)
These dramatic foliage plants have large wavy leaves margined with silver and with a pronounced metallic sheen
☼ Filtered light 🌡 No lower than 15°C (59°F) in winter 💧 Apply a balanced fertilizer every 2–3 weeks when in growth 💧 Freely in spring and summer, moderately in winter ▭ Loam-based potting compost with added sand and composted bark

Aloe aristata *Lace aloe*
Height to 12cm (5in), spread 12cm (5in)
These succulents have thick, pointed leaves with pronounced white spots
☼ Full light 🌡 No lower than 10°C (50°F) in winter 💧 Apply a balanced fertilizer every 8 weeks in spring and summer 💧 Moderately throughout the year, but sparingly when dormant ▭ Standard potting compost with added sharp sand or perlite

Aloe variegata *Partridge-breasted aloe*
Height to 20cm (8in), spread 20cm (8in)
Succulents with thick, fleshy leaves broadly banded with silver
☼ Full light 🌡 No lower than 10°C (50°F) in winter 💧 Apply a balanced fertilizer every 8 weeks in spring and summer 💧 Moderately throughout the year, but sparingly when dormant ▭ Standard potting compost with added sharp sand or perlite

Aloe vera
Height to 60cm (24in), spread 60cm (24in)
Widely used in the cosmetics industry, this succulent also makes an attractive houseplant. It is tolerant of a certain amount of neglect
☼ Full light 🌡 No lower than 10°C (50°F) in winter 💧 Apply a balanced fertilizer every 8 weeks in spring and summer 💧 Moderately throughout the year, but sparingly when dormant ▭ Standard potting compost with added sharp sand or perlite

Aphelandra squarrosa *Zebra plant*
Height to 30cm (12in), spread 30cm (12in)
This dramatic houseplant is grown for its white-ribbed leaves and spikes of yellow flowers
☼ Full light, filtered in summer 🌡 No lower than 7°C (45°F) in winter, but better kept warmer 💧 Feed with a balanced fertilizer every 2 weeks in summer, every 4 weeks in winter 💧 Apply soft water freely when in growth, more sparingly in winter ▭ Standard potting compost

Aspidistra elatior *Cast-iron plant*
Height to 60cm (24in), spread 60cm (24in)
Among the easiest houseplants to grow, aspidistras are tough plants that seem to withstand any amount of neglect
☼ Bright filtered light, but tolerates shadier positions 🌡 Ideally no lower than 7°C (45°F) in winter 💧 Apply a balanced fertilizer every 4 weeks when in growth 💧 Moderately when in growth, sparingly in winter ▭ Standard potting compost

Asplenium nidus *Bird's nest fern*
Height to 1.5m (5ft), spread 1m (3ft)
These ferns have glossy, strap-like leaves that curl at the tips
☼ Bright filtered light 🌡 No lower than 10°C (50°F) in winter 💧 Apply a balanced fertilizer at half strength every 4 weeks when in growth 💧 Freely when in growth, sparingly in winter ▭ Standard potting compost with added peat substitute, sharp sand, and charcoal

Begonia x tuberhybrida *Tuberhybrida begonia*
Height and spread variable depending on the variety grown; some have trailing stems and are good in hanging baskets
Tuberous begonias, which are completely dormant in winter, are grown for their luminous flowers in shades of white, pink, yellow, orange, and red over a long period in summer to early autumn
☼ Bright light with shade from direct sun 🌡 Store in a frost-free place when dormant in winter 💧 Apply a balanced fertilizer every second watering when in growth 💧 Freely when in growth; keep dry in winter ▭ Standard potting compost

Begonia 'Norah Bedson'
Height to 23cm (9in), spread 25cm (10in)
A so-called rhizomatous begonia, this has red-speckled stems and mottled leaves
☼ Bright light with shade from direct sun 🌡 No lower than 10°C (50°F) in winter 💧 Apply a balanced fertilizer every second watering when in growth 💧 Freely when in growth; keep dry in winter ▭ Standard potting compost

Begonia (rex-cultorum types) *Painted-leaf begonia*
Height to 60cm (24in), spread 60cm (24in), depending on the species
Rex begonias are grown for their brilliantly coloured leaves, which often have a metallic sheen. The flowers are inconspicuous

☼ Bright light with shade from direct sun ≣ No lower than 10°C (50°F) in winter ♦ Apply a balanced fertilizer every second watering when in growth ◊ Freely when in growth; keep dry in winter ⊟ Standard potting compost

Blechnum species *Hard fern*
Height and spread depend on the species but usually to 30cm (12in) when grown as a houseplant
These handsome ferns appreciate high humidity so make a good choice for a kitchen or bathroom. In time, they develop a woody stem at the crown
☼ Bright filtered or indirect light ≣ No lower than 18°C (64°F) in winter ♦ Not necessary ◊ Water freely when in growth, moderately in winter ⊟ Standard potting compost with added bark, charcoal, and sharp sand

Bougainvillea hybrids *Paper flower*
Height to 5m (15ft), spread 5m (15ft), less in a container
These showy climbers are grown not for their true flowers, which are inconspicuous, but for the white, pink, red, or salmon orange bracts that surround them. They are best given some support. The stems are thorny
☼ Full light ≣ No lower than 0°C (32°F) in winter ♦ Apply a balanced fertilizer every 4 weeks when in growth ◊ Water freely when in growth, and keep just moist in winter ⊟ Standard potting compost

Bouvardia hybrids
Height to 90cm (36in), spread 60cm (24in)
These shrubby plants usually flower from late summer into winter. Some varieties have scented flowers
☼ Bright filtered light ≣ No lower than 5°C (41°F) in winter ♦ Apply a balanced fertilizer every 4 weeks when in growth, but not when flowering ◊ Water freely when in growth, keep just moist in winter ⊟ Standard potting compost

Brassica oleracea *Ornamental cabbage*
Height to 45cm (18in), spread to 45cm (18in)
Ornamental cabbages and kales are annual plants that are at their best in autumn and winter. They colour best at low temperatures, so keep them outdoors for most of the time, bringing them inside for short spells only
☼ Bright light with shade from direct sun ≣ Ideally below 10°C (50°F); higher temperatures are tolerated for short periods ♦ Apply a balanced fertilizer every 4 weeks when in growth ◊ Freely when in growth ⊟ Standard potting compost

CACTI
Height to 30cm (12in), spread 15cm (6in), but depends on the species and the age of the plant
Desert cacti are grown for the fascination of their overall appearance. Some are tall and slender, others almost globular, and nearly all are spiny. Not all will flower as young plants. Most are slow-growing
☼ Full light ≣ No lower than 7°C (45°F) in winter, though some will tolerate short spells at near freezing ♦ When in growth, apply cactus fertilizer every 4–5 weeks ◊ In growth, soak thoroughly with soft water and allow to dry out between waterings; keep dry in winter ⊟ Cactus compost

Calathea species
Height and spread variable depending on the species, but usually within 1m (3ft).
These foliage plants are adapted to low light levels, so make excellent houseplants. They need high humidity
☼ Bright indirect or filtered light ≣ No lower than 16°C (61°F) in winter ♦ Apply a balanced liquid fertilizer every 4 weeks when in growth ◊ Freely when in growth, moderately in winter; mist daily ⊟ Standard potting compost

Campanula isophylla *Falling stars*
Height to 20cm (8in), spread 30cm (12in)
With numerous light blue or white flowers in mid-summer, these make excellent subjects for pots and hanging baskets
☼ Bright filtered light ≣ No lower than 0°C (32°F) in winter ♦ In growth, apply a balanced feed every 4 weeks ◊ In growth, water freely; keep moist in winter ⊟ Standard potting compost

Capsicum annuum *Chilli pepper, paprika*
Height to 30cm (12in), spread 30cm (12in)
Apart from their uses in the kitchen, these make attractive indoor plants, with their showy white, yellow, orange, red, or purple fruits
☼ Bright filtered light ≣ No lower than 4°C (39°F) in winter ♦ Feed with a balanced fertilizer every 10 days when in growth until the fruits start to colour ◊ Water freely when in growth, sparingly in winter ⊟ Standard potting compost

Chlorophytum comosum 'Vittatum' *Spider plant*
Height to 20cm (8in) or more, spread 30cm (12in) or more
These familiar plants are extremely tolerant and will grow in a variety of situations; they are excellent in hanging baskets

☼ Bright indirect to full light, but shaded from hot sun ≣ No lower than 7°C (45°F) in winter ♦ Apply a green foliage plant fertilizer every 4 weeks when in growth ◊ Water freely when in growth, moderately in winter ⊟ Standard potting compost

Citrus species *Orange, lemon, lime, etc.*
Height to 2m (6ft), spread 1m (3ft)
These evergreen shrubs have intoxicatingly scented flowers that open at the same time as the previous year's fruits are ripening. Plants can be clipped over to keep them within bounds
☼ Full light, but shaded from hot sun ≣ No lower than 3°C (37°F) in winter ♦ Apply balanced liquid fertilizer every 2–3 weeks when in growth ◊ In growth water freely and mist daily; water sparingly in winter ⊟ Standard potting compost

Clivia miniata *Kaffir lily*
Height to 45cm (18in), spread 30cm (12in)
Among the easiest flowering houseplants to grow, clivias have showy orange flowers in spring, carried on strong stems above the arching, strap-like leaves. They flower best when pot-bound
☼ Bright filtered or indirect light ≣ No lower than 10°C (50°F) in winter ♦ Apply a balanced fertilizer every 4 weeks when in growth (but not when the flower buds are forming) ◊ Freely when in growth, moderately in winter ⊟ Standard potting compost with added grit or perlite

Codiaeum hybrids *Croton*
Height to 90cm (36in), spread 60cm (24in)
These houseplants are grown for their brilliantly coloured, leathery leaves. The flowers are inconspicuous
☼ Full light with shade from hot sun ≣ No lower than 8°C (46°F) in winter ♦ In growth, apply a balanced fertilizer every 2–3 weeks ◊ In growth, water freely and mist daily; water sparingly in winter with tepid water ⊟ Standard potting compost

Convallaria majalis *Lily-of-the-valley*
Height to 23cm (9in), spread 30cm (12in)
Lily-of-the-valley is a hardy garden plant that can be forced in containers to produce its deliciously scented flowers indoors in late winter. Pot plants up in autumn; return to the garden after flowering
☼ Bright indirect light ≣ No lower than 0°C (32°F) in winter ♦ Apply a flowering houseplant fertilizer when in growth until the flower buds form ◊ Freely when in growth ⊟ Standard potting compost

Cyclamen persicum hybrids *Florists' cyclamen*

Height to 20cm (8in), spread 15cm (6in)

These cyclamen have been bred as houseplants that flower in autumn and winter. The flowers, which have distinctive swept-back petals, can be white, pink, glowing red, or purple. They appreciate cool conditions

☼ Bright filtered light, full light in winter ❄ No lower than 13°C (55°F) in winter ♠ Flowering houseplant fertilizer every 2 weeks when in leaf ◊ Freely when in growth (but not directly over the tuber); keep dry when dormant in summer ▦ Standard potting compost

Cyperus involucratus *Umbrella grass*

Height to 60cm (24in), spread 60cm (24in)

This grassy plant grows in water in the wild, but is eminently suitable for growing as a houseplant if given sufficient moisture

☼ Bright filtered light ❄ No lower than 5°C (41°F) in winter ♠ Apply a balanced fertilizer every 4 weeks in summer ◊ Water freely and stand containers in shallow trays of water ▦ Standard potting compost

Dendrobium hybrids

Height to 60cm (24in), spread 30cm (12in)

These orchids are mainly spring-flowering

☼ Lightly shaded from late spring to summer; full light from autumn to early spring ❄ No lower than 10°C (50°F) in winter ♠ Apply an orchid fertilizer at every 3rd watering when in growth ◊ When in growth, water freely and mist twice daily; keep dry in winter ▦ Epiphytic orchid compost

Dieffenbachia seguine 'Exotica' *Dumb cane*

Height to 1m (3ft), spread 40cm (16in)

The large leaves of this plant are generously splashed and mottled with creamy white. It is one of a large number of selected forms of the species

☼ Bright filtered light; full light in winter ❄ No lower than 15°C (59°F) in winter ♠ In growth, apply a balanced fertilizer every 4 weeks ◊ In growth, water moderately and mist daily; water sparingly in winter ▦ Standard potting compost

Dracaena fragrans Deremensis Group

Height to 5m (15ft), spread 1m (3ft), often less in a container

These shrubby plants branch with age and can become tree-like. They are grown for their strikingly variegated leaves

☼ Full light, shaded from direct sun ❄ No lower than 13°C (55°F) in winter ♠ From spring to autumn, apply a balanced fertilizer every 4 weeks ◊ Freely when in growth, sparingly in winter ▦ Standard potting compost

Echeveria species

Height to 15cm (6in), spread 30cm (12in), depending on the species

These succulents form rosettes of fleshy leaves. The tall, arching flower spikes are of secondary interest

☼ Full light ❄ No lower than 7°C (45°F) in winter ♠ In growth, apply a balanced fertilizer at half strength every 4 weeks ◊ In growth, water moderately; keep just moist in winter ▦ Cactus compost

Euphorbia abyssinica

Height to 1.2m (4ft), spread 45cm (18in)

This almost tree-like succulent looks like a cactus, with its curious angled stems

☼ Full light ❄ No lower than 12°C (54°F) in winter ♠ In growth, apply a balanced fertilizer at half strength every 2 weeks ◊ In growth, water moderately; keep just moist in winter ▦ Standard potting compost with added grit

Fatshedera lizei *Tree ivy*

Height to 1.2m (4ft), spread 3m (10ft)

These tolerant shrubs (hybrids of fatsia and ivy) are actually hardy enough to be grown outdoors in most climates, but also make dramatic houseplants

☼ Most situations are acceptable, but shade from hot summer sun ❄ Tree ivies will survive lows of -5°C (23°F) ♠ In growth, apply a balanced fertilizer every 4 weeks ◊ Freely when in growth, sparingly in winter ▦ Standard potting compost

Ficus benjamina *Weeping fig*

Height to 1.5m (5ft), spread 1.2m (4ft)

Easily grown shrubs that, given the right conditions, can exceed the dimensions given here

☼ Full or filtered light ❄ No lower than 15°C (59°F) ♠ In growth, apply a green foliage plant fertilizer every 4 weeks ◊ Freely when in growth, moderately at other times ▦ Standard potting compost with added fine bark chippings

Ficus lyrata *Banjo fig, fiddle-leaf fig*

Height to 2m (6ft), spread 45cm (18in)

This foliage plant has fiddle-shaped, glossy green leaves that are roughly corrugated. An excellent foil to flowering plants

☼ Bright or filtered light ❄ No lower than 15°C (59°F) in winter ♠ In growth, apply a foliage houseplant fertilizer every 4 weeks ◊ Freely when in growth, moderately at other times ▦ Standard potting compost with added fine bark chippings

Gardenia augusta *Gardenia*

Height to 45cm (18in), spread 45cm (18in)

The glossy, rich green leaves offset the sweetly scented, white flowers in summer and autumn

☼ Bright filtered light ❄ No lower than 10°C (50°F) in winter ♠ In growth, apply a balanced fertilizer every 4 weeks ◊ In growth, water freely with soft water; keep barely moist in winter ▦ Ericaceous potting compost

Gerbera jamesonii hybrids *Transvaal daisy*

Height to 45cm (18in), spread 60cm (24in)

These plants have long-lasting, brilliantly coloured daisy flowers (cream, yellow, apricot, orange, and pink) over a long period from spring to autumn but are sometimes forced to flower at other times of year.

☼ Bright filtered light ❄ No lower than 5°C (41°F) in winter ♠ In growth, apply a balanced fertilizer every 4 weeks ◊ Water freely when in growth; keep moist in winter ▦ Standard potting compost

Guzmania lingulata *Scarlet star*

Height to 45cm (18in), spread 45cm (18in)

In winter, this bromeliad has brilliant orange-red or scarlet bracts that surround the true flowers

☼ Bright filtered or indirect light ❄ No lower than 15°C (59°F) in winter ♠ None required ◊ In growth, mist daily with soft water; in winter, keep the compost barely moist and do not mist ▦ Bromeliad compost

Hibiscus rosa-sinensis hybrids *Rose of China*

Height to 1.5m (5ft), spread 1m (3ft)

These fast-growing shrubs have bright glossy green leaves and flowers in shades of crimson, orange, yellow, and white

☼ Bright filtered light ❄ No lower than 10°C (50°F) in winter ♠ In growth, apply a balanced fertilizer every 4 weeks ◊ Freely when in growth, sparingly in winter ▦ Standard potting compost

Hippeastrum hybrids *Amaryllis*

Height to 30–50cm (12–20in), spread 30cm (12in)

These bulbs are usually forced to flower in late winter. Flower colours include white, pink, and red; selected forms can have double or bi-coloured flowers

☼ Bright filtered or full light ❄ No lower than 13°C (55°F) in winter ♠ Feed with a balanced fertilizer every 2 weeks after flowering until the leaves start to die back ◊ Freely when in growth; keep dry when dormant ▦ Standard potting compost or bulb fibre; plant with the neck of the bulb above the compost surface

Howea fosteriana *Kentia palm*

Height to 2.5m (8ft), spread 2m (6ft)

These dramatic-looking palms seem to thrive in a variety of positions in the home and are apparently indestructible

☼ Full light ❄ No lower than 15°C (59°F) in winter

In growth, apply a balanced fertilizer monthly
Moderately when in active growth, sparingly at other times Standard potting compost

Hyacinthus orientalis hybrids *Hyacinth*
Height to 30cm (12in), spread 8cm (3in)
With deliciously scented flowers in shades of white, pink, blue, purple, red, and salmon orange, hyacinths retain their popularity. Specially prepared bulbs have been forced to flower in winter. After flowering, they can be planted in the garden, but may take a season or two to recover
Keep bulbs for forcing in the dark for 6 weeks until the shoots are 2.5cm (1in) long, then bring them into full light No higher than 7°C (45°F) when kept dark; then at room temperature
None necessary Water carefully to avoid waterlogging the shoots Bulb fibre

Hydrangea macrophylla hybrids *Hydrangea*
Height to 1m (3ft), spread 1m (3ft)
These hardy shrubs normally flower in mid-summer, but are often forced into flower at other times and sold as houseplants. They are unsuitable for growing indoors indefinitely: after flowering, cut them back and keep them in containers outdoors or plant them in the open garden
Bright indirect light No lower than 0°C (32°F) Slow-release fertilizer after flowering
Water freely while in active growth Standard potting compost

Isolepis cernua (syn. Scirpus cernuus) *Slender club-rush*
Height to 20cm (8in), spread 45cm (18in)
This grass-like plant is usually trailing and is therefore suitable for a hanging basket, but can be trimmed back with scissors for a neater appearance
Bright filtered light No lower than 10°C (50°F) in winter In growth, apply a green houseplant fertilizer every 4 weeks Water freely in growth; keep moist in winter Standard potting compost

Jasminum polyanthum *Jasmine*
Height to 1m (3ft), spread 60cm (2ft), but depends on the support used
This climber has deliciously fragrant flowers in late winter to early spring. Though delicate-looking, it is surprisingly vigorous. It needs some support – a hoop of either cane or wire is best
Bright filtered light or full light with shade from hot sun No lower than 0°C (32°F) in winter
In growth, apply a flowering houseplant fertilizer every 4 weeks In growth, water freely, sparingly in winter Standard potting compost

Juncus effusus 'Spiralis' *Corkscrew rush*
Height to 45cm (18in), spread 60cm (24in)
This bizarre plant is grown for the appeal of its spiralling, shiny dark green stems
Full light No lower than 0°C (32°F) in winter
Apply a balanced fertilizer every 4 weeks when in growth Water freely throughout the year to keep permanently moist Standard potting compost

Kalanchoe daigremontiana *Mexican hat plant*
Height to 1m (3ft), spread 30cm (12in)
This succulent has fleshy grey leaves with toothed margins, but its principal attraction is its method of reproduction – tiny new plantlets are produced all along the leaf edges
Bright filtered light No lower than 10°C (50°F) in winter Apply a balanced liquid fertilizer every 4 weeks when in active growth Freely from spring to autumn, keep just moist in winter Standard potting compost with added grit

Kalanchoe hybrids *Flaming Katy*
Height to 30cm (12in), spread 30cm (12in)
Familiar plants with glossy, succulent-looking green leaves and clusters of red, yellow, pink, or orange flowers in winter and spring
Bright filtered light No lower than 10°C (50°F) in winter Apply a balanced liquid fertilizer every 4 weeks when in active growth Freely from spring to autumn, keep just moist in winter Standard potting compost with added grit

Kalanchoe thyrsiflora
Height to 60cm (24in), spread 30cm (12in)
This succulent has red-margined, pale green leaves and clusters of fragrant yellow flowers in spring
Bright filtered light No lower than 12°C (54°F) in winter Apply a balanced liquid fertilizer every 4 weeks when in active growth Freely from spring to autumn, keep just moist in winter Standard potting compost with added grit

Lavandula species *Lavender*
Height to 60cm (2ft), spread 45cm (18in)
A number of different lavenders are grown, all with narrow, characteristically aromatic, grey-green leaves and lavender, pink, or white flowers
Full light In a container, no lower than 0°C (32°F) in winter Apply a balanced fertilizer every 4 weeks when in growth Water freely when in growth, keep just moist in winter Standard potting compost with added grit or perlite

Medinilla magnifica *Rose grape*
Height to 2m (6ft), spread 1.5m (5ft)
Exotic-looking shrubs with glossy, strongly ribbed leaves and showy, pink to coral-red flowers

Bright filtered light or full light with shade from hot sun No lower than 15°C (59°F) in winter
In growth, apply a balanced fertilizer every 4 weeks Moderately when in growth, sparingly in winter Standard potting compost

Monstera deliciosa *Swiss cheese plant*
Height to 3m (10ft), spread 1m (3ft)
This impressive foliage plant is actually a robust climber that can exceed the dimensions given if the conditions suit it
Bright indirect light No lower than 15°C (59°F) in winter In growth, apply a green houseplant fertilizer every 4 weeks In growth, water freely and mist twice daily; water sparingly in winter Standard potting compost

Narcissus hybrids *Daffodil*
Height to 35cm (14in), spread to 15cm (6in)
These delightful spring bulbs should be grown in containers outdoors and brought inside once the flower buds have formed
Full light No lower than 0°C (32°F) in winter
Apply a balanced fertilizer immediately after flowering Water freely without flooding the compost Bulb fibre

Nephrolepis exaltata 'Bostoniensis' *Boston fern*
Height to 1m (3ft), spread 1m (3ft)
The Boston fern makes a tolerant houseplant, with fronds that are erect at first, then arch over
Bright filtered light No lower than 7°C (45°F) in winter In growth, apply a balanced fertilizer at half strength every 4 weeks In full growth, water moderately with soft water and mist twice daily; water sparingly in winter Standard compost with added sharp sand

Nertera granadensis *Bead plant*
Height to 2cm (¾in), spread 20cm (8in)
The principal attraction of this trailing plant is its shining, bead-like, orange or red berries that ripen in late summer
Bright filtered or indirect light No lower than 0°C (32°F) in winter In growth, apply a balanced fertilizer every 4 weeks In growth, water freely, sparingly in winter Loamless potting compost

Ocimum basilicum *Basil*
Height to 30cm (12in), spread 30cm (12in)
This important culinary herb is essential for many Mediterranean, Indian, and Fusion dishes. It is generally grown as an annual
Full light with shade from hot sun No lower than 0°C (32°F) in winter Apply a balanced fertilizer when in growth Water freely
Standard potting compost

Olea europea *Olive*

Height to 2m (6ft), spread 1.5m (5ft)

Familiar throughout the Mediterranean, where it is an important economic plant, the olive is an increasingly popular subject for a conservatory, though the olives are unlikely to ripen fully

☼ Full light ◫ Ideally no lower than 0°C (32°F) in winter, though short cold dry spells are tolerated ◔ In growth apply a balanced fertilizer every 4 weeks ◇ Moderately when in growth, sparingly in winter ▭ Standard potting compost

Ophiopogon planiscapus 'Nigrescens'
Black grass

Height to 20cm (8in), spread to 30cm (12in)

This grass is a hardy plant that is grown for its unique, blackish purple leaves. It is best kept in a container outdoors and brought inside for short spells only

☼ Bright light with shade from direct sun ◫ Will tolerate lows of -15°C (5°F) outdoors ◔ Apply a balanced fertilizer every 4 weeks when in growth ◇ Freely when in growth ▭ Standard potting compost

Origanum species *Marjoram, oregano*

Height and spread usually to 30cm (12in), but depends on the species

These aromatic herbs have wide culinary use as well as charming, lilac, pink, or mauve flowers

☼ Full light with shade from hot sun ◫ In a container, no lower than 0°C (32°F) in winter ◔ In growth, apply a balanced fertilizer every 4 weeks ◇ Moderately when in growth, sparingly in winter ▭ Standard potting compost

Paphiopedilum hybrids *Slipper orchid*

Height to 30cm (12in), spread 20cm (8in)

These orchids are becoming increasingly widely grown as houseplants and many attractive hybrids have been developed, most flowering in winter for up to 10 weeks or more

☼ Bright filtered light in summer; full light in winter ◫ No lower than 13°C (55°F) in winter ◔ In growth, apply an orchid fertilizer at every 3rd watering ◇ In growth, water freely and mist twice daily; in winter, water sparingly but do not allow the compost to dry out between waterings ▭ Terrestrial orchid compost in containers that restrict the roots

Pennisetum species *Fountain grass*

Height and spread to 60cm (24in), depending on the species

Most of these grasses are hardy perennials that are best grown in containers outdoors and brought inside for short spells only

☼ Full light with shade from hot sun ◫ In a container, no lower than 0°C (32°F) in winter ◔ In growth, apply a balanced fertilizer every 4 weeks ◇ In growth, water freely, sparingly in winter ▭ Standard potting compost

Phalaenposis hybrids *Moth orchid*

Height to 1m (3ft), spread 60cm (2ft)

These beautiful orchids have been specially bred to tolerate the dry atmosphere of most centrally heated living rooms. The arching stems of flowers are of unmatched elegance and can be produced throughout the year. They are a popular choice for bridal bouquets

☼ Bright filtered light ◫ No lower than 18°C (64°F) in winter ◔ Apply an orchid fertilizer every 4 weeks from spring to autumn ◇ From spring to autumn, water freely and mist twice daily; in winter, water sparingly and do not mist ▭ Epiphytic orchid compost

Philodendron erubescens *Blushing philodendron*

Height to 2m (6ft), spread 30cm (12in), depending on how it is trained

This attractive climber has glossy, heart-shaped leaves. As a houseplant, it is best trained up a moss pole

☼ Bright filtered or indirect light ◫ No lower than 15°C (59°F) in winter ◔ In growth, apply a green houseplant fertilizer every 4 weeks ◇ Water freely when in growth, sparingly in winter ▭ Loamless potting compost

Pogonatherum saccharoideum *House bamboo*

Height to 60cm (24in), spread 60cm (24in)

Most bamboos are large, colonizing plants, but the so-called house bamboo is an exception that makes a delightful houseplant

☼ Full light with shade from hot sun ◫ No lower than 15°C (59°F) in winter ◔ In growth, apply a balanced fertilizer every 4 weeks ◇ Water freely in active growth, only moderately in winter; the compost should never dry out ▭ Standard potting compost

Primula obconica *Poison primrose*

Height to 30cm (12in), spread 25cm (8in)

One of the prettiest of flowering houseplants for winter and spring, this primula is suitable for any cool area in the house such as a bedroom or hallway. The rough, hairy leaves can irritate the skin

☼ Bright filtered light ◫ No lower than 0°C (32°F) in winter, though short spells at cooler temperatures are tolerated ◔ In growth, apply a balanced fertilizer at half strength every week ◇ Water freely when in growth, sparingly at other times ▭ Standard potting compost with added grit or perlite

Rosa hybrids *Rose*

Height to 1.2m (4ft), spread 1m (3ft), depending on the variety

Roses that are suitable for containers can be brought into the house for short spells as soon as the buds show colour. After flowering, return them out of doors

☼ Full light with shade from hot sun ◫ In a container, no lower than -5°C (23°F) in winter, though cooler temperatures can be tolerated ◔ Apply a balanced fertilizer when in growth ◇ Water freely when in growth; keep barely moist at other times ▭ Standard potting compost

Saintpaulia hybrids *African violet*

Height to 15–20cm (6–8in), spread 15–20cm (6–8in)

With clustered flowers in shades of white, pink, purple, magenta, and violet produced throughout the year, African violets are among the best flowering houseplants

☼ Bright filtered light ◫ No lower than 15°C (59°F) in winter ◔ Apply special Saintpaulia fertilizer throughout the year ◇ Water throughout the year to keep the compost moist and mist daily when in active growth ▭ Loamless potting compost. Repot only when the roots fill the pot

Sansevieria trifasciata 'Laurentii' *Mother-in-law's tongue*

Height to 1m (3ft), spread 30cm (12in)

With their boldly marked, upright leaves, these plants make a strong statement wherever they are placed

☼ Bright filtered or indirect light ◫ No lower than 13°C (55°F) in winter ◔ In growth, apply a balanced fertilizer at half strength every 4 weeks ◇ Freely when in full growth, sparingly in winter ▭ Standard potting compost with added grit

Schefflera elegantissima *False aralia*

Height to 2m (6ft), spread 1m (3ft)

This dramatic plant has strikingly toothed leaf margins

☼ Bright filtered or indirect light ◫ No lower than 13°C (55°F) in winter ◔ In growth, apply a balanced fertilizer every 4 weeks ◇ Moderately when in growth, keep just moist in winter ▭ Standard potting compost

Schlumbergera hybrids *Christmas cactus*

Height to 30cm (12in), spread 30cm (12in)

These rainforest cacti flower annually in autumn to winter when grown as houseplants

☼ Bright indirect light ◫ No lower than 10°C (50°F) in winter ◔ In growth, apply a flowering houseplant fertilizer every 4 weeks ◇ Water moderately when in full growth and mist daily; keep the compost just moist for up to 8 weeks after flowering to allow the plants to rest ▭ Epiphytic cactus compost

Scutellaria costaricana *Skullcap*

Height to 50cm (20in), spread 50cm (20in)

These shrubby plants produce spikes of fiery red flowers in summer. They have often been treated with a growth inhibitor to keep them compact

☼ Bright filtered light ≡ No lower than 15˚C (59˚F) in winter ♦ In growth, apply a balanced fertilizer every 4 weeks ◊ Water freely when in growth, keep just moist in winter ▨ Standard potting compost

Senecio rowleyanus *String of beads*

Height to 60cm (24in), spread indefinite

This trailing plant, whose stems will root where they touch the compost surface, has spherical, bright green leaves. It is excellent in a hanging basket

☼ Full light ≡ No lower than 7˚C (45˚F) in winter ♦ In growth, apply a balanced fertilizer at half strength every 4 weeks ◊ Water moderately when in growth, keep just moist in winter ▨ Standard potting compost with added grit

Solanum pseudocapsicum *Jerusalem cherry*

Height to 30cm (12in), spread 30cm (12in)

These shrubs are grown for their marble-like, red, yellow, or orange fruits. They are often treated as annuals and discarded after fruiting

☼ Full light with shade from hot sun, or bright filtered light ≡ No lower than 5˚C (41˚F) in winter ♦ Apply a flowering houseplant fertilizer every 2–3 weeks until the fruits begin to ripen ◊ Water freely when in growth and mist daily; water sparingly when dormant after fruiting ▨ Standard potting compost

Soleirolia soleirolii *Baby's tears, mind-your-own-business*

Height to 10cm (4in), spread indefinite

This spreading plant, with its tiny green leaves, is often used as ground cover in gardens. In pots, it makes appealing domes of foliage if several plants are massed together. Trim with scissors to keep neat

☼ Full light with shade from hot sun, or partial shade ≡ No lower than 0˚C (32˚F) in winter ♦ In growth, apply a balanced fertilizer at half strength every 4 weeks ◊ In growth, water freely, sparingly in winter ▨ Standard potting compost with added grit

Spathiphyllum wallisii *Peace lily*

Height to 90cm (36in), spread 90cm (36in)

These elegant plants produce their arum-like flowers throughout the summer

☼ Bright indirect light ≡ No lower than 10˚C (50˚F) in winter ♦ In growth, apply a balanced fertilizer every 4 weeks ◊ In growth, water freely and mist daily; keep just moist in winter ▨ Standard potting compost

Stephanotis floribunda *Wax flower*

Height to 3m (10ft), spread 3m (10ft), depending on the support

These climbers, producing intoxicatingly scented flowers from spring to autumn, can be trained on hoops of wire inserted in the pot, or, where there is more room, on a trellis

☼ Full light with shade from hot sun ≡ No lower than 15˚C (59˚F) in winter ♦ In growth, apply a balanced fertilizer every 2–3 weeks ◊ In growth, water and mist freely; water sparingly in winter ▨ Standard potting compost

Tacca chantrierei *Bat flower, cat's whiskers, devil flower*

Height to 1m (3ft), spread 1m (3ft)

Among the huge, wrinkled leaves the sinister-looking green, brown, or black flowers, with thread-like appendages, make their appearance in summer

☼ Bright filtered light ≡ No lower than 13˚C (55˚F) in winter ♦ In summer, spray with a foliar fertilizer at half strength every 4 weeks ◊ Water and mist freely throughout the year ▨ Mix of leaf mould and coarse bark with added slow-release fertilizer

Thymus species *Thyme*

Height to 15cm (6in), spread to 30cm (12in), depending on the species

These aromatic sub-shrubs are grown mainly for culinary use, but also have the attraction of white, lilac, or purple flowers in summer, which are very attractive to bees. They can also be planted outdoors in the cracks in paving

☼ Full light ≡ In a container, no lower than 0˚C (32˚F) in winter, though short spells at cooler temperatures are tolerated ♦ In growth, apply a balanced fertilizer every 4 weeks ◊ In growth, water freely, moderately in winter ▨ Standard potting compost with added grit or perlite

Tillandsia wagneriana *Air plant*

Height to 40cm (16in), spread 45cm (18in)

This bromeliad is grown for its strap-like, curved, bright green leaves and its pink flowers, produced in spring or autumn

☼ Bright filtered light ≡ No lower than 7˚C (45˚F) in winter ♦ In growth, apply a flowering houseplant fertilizer at half strength every 4 weeks ◊ In growth, water freely; keep just moist in winter ▨ Terrestrial bromeliad compost

Tradescantia fluminensis 'Albovittata'

Wandering Jew

Height to 15cm (6in), spread 20cm (8in)

This familiar houseplant is easy to grow. Its trailing habit makes it ideal for massing in a hanging basket

☼ Bright filtered light ≡ No lower than 10˚C

(50˚F) in winter ♦ In growth, apply a balanced fertilizer every 4 weeks ◊ In growth, water freely, sparingly in winter ▨ Standard potting compost

Tradescantia zebrina *Wandering Jew*

Height to 15cm (6in), spread 20cm (8in)

This trailing plant has pointed, bluish green leaves that are strongly striped with luminous silver. The three-petalled, purple-pink flowers, of lesser ornamental value, can be produced at any time during the year

☼ Bright filtered light ≡ No lower than 10˚C (50˚F) in winter ♦ In growth, apply a balanced fertilizer every 4 weeks ◊ In growth water freely, sparingly in winter ▨ Standard potting compost

Viola x wittrockiana *Pansy*

Height to 23cm (9in), spread to 30cm (12in)

Pansies are universally popular with their mask-like "faces". They appreciate cool conditions, so keep them outdoors and bring them inside for short spells only. Plants are raised to flower at varying times of the year: winter-flowering pansies are especially welcome

☼ Full light with shade from hot sun ≡ Pansies will tolerate freezing temperatures ♦ Apply a flowering houseplant fertilizer every 2 weeks until the flower buds have formed ◊ Water freely, but avoid waterlogging the compost ▨ Standard potting compost

Vuylstekeara Cambria 'Plush'

Height to 1.2m (4ft), spread 60cm (2ft)

One of the least demanding orchids, this hybrid has tall, branching spikes of rust-red flowers that can appear at any time of year

☼ Bright filtered light when in active growth; full light in winter ≡ No lower than 10˚C (50˚F) in winter ♦ In growth, apply orchid fertilizer at every 3rd watering ◊ Water freely when in growth and mist twice daily; water sparingly in winter ▨ Epiphytic orchid compost

Zantedeschia hybrids *Arum lily*

Height to 90cm (36in), spread 60cm (24in)

Beautiful plants with shiny green leaves, flowering in spring to early summer. The elegant spathes (the true flowers inside are inconspicuous) are usually white, though yellow, pink, red, or purple varieties are also available. Some species are hardy and can be grown outdoors

☼ Full light ≡ No lower than 10˚C (50˚F) in winter ♦ In growth, apply a balanced fertilizer every 2 weeks until the flowers have faded ◊ In growth, water freely, keep just moist in winter ▨ Standard potting compost

USEFUL ADDRESSES

Abbotsbury Sub-tropical Gardens
Abbotsbury
Nr. Weymouth
Dorset DT3 4LA
(01305) 871344
Tender plants from Australia,
New Zealand, and South Africa

Architectural Plants
Cooks Farm
Nuthurst
Horsham
West Sussex RH13 6LH
(01403) 891772
Olives

**Architectural Plants
(Chichester) Ltd**
Lidsey Road Nursery
Westergate
Nr. Chichester
West Sussex PO20 6SU
(01243) 545008
http://members.aol.com/gshaw29868/
archplnt.htm

Aria
295–296 Upper Street
London N1 2TU
(020) 7704 1999
www.ariashop.co.uk
Modern pots and containers

Bridgemere Nurseries
Bridgemere
Nr. Nantwich
Cheshire CW5 7QB
(01270) 521100
Houseplants

Brookside Nursery
Elderberry Farm
Bognor Road
Rowhook
Horsham
West Sussex RH12 3PS
(01403) 790996
www.cactus-mall.com/nursery/brooksid.html
Cacti and succulents

**Burncoose and South Down
Nurseries**
Redruth
Cornwall TR16 6BJ
(01209) 860316
www.eclipse.co.uk/burncoose
Conservatory plants

Burnham Nurseries
Forches Cross
Newton Abbot
Devon TQ12 6PZ
(01626) 352233
www.eclipse.co.uk/burnhamorchids
Orchids

Carden Cunietti
83 Westbourne Park Road
London W2 5QH
(020) 7229 8630
www.carden//cunietti.com
One-off items, unusual boxes
and containers

Ceramica Blue
10 Blenheim Crescent
London W11 1NN
(020) 7727 0288
Handmade ceramics

Cheshire Herbs
Fourfields
Forest Road
Nr. Tarporley
Cheshire CW6 9ES
(01829) 760578

Chessington Nurseries Ltd
Leatherhead Road
Chessington
Surrey KT19 2NG
(01372) 725638
Conservatory plants

Conservatory PlantLine
Nayland Road
West Bergholt
Colchester
Essex CO6 3DH
(01206) 242533
www.scarletts.org

Designers Guild
267 Kings Road
London SW3 2NA
www.designersguild.com
(020) 7351 5775

Dibleys Nurseries
Llanelidan
Ruthin
North Wales LL15 2LG
(01978) 790677
www.dibleys.com
Unusual houseplants

Earth Tones
36 Trent Avenue
London W5 4TL
(020) 8354 0333
www.earthtones.co.uk
Soft furnishings and containers

Fibrex Nurseries Ltd
Honeybourne Road
Pebworth
Stratford-on-Avon
Warwickshire CV37 8XP
(01789) 720788
Pelargoniums

Flora Exotica
Pasadena
South-Green
Fingringhoe
Colchester
Essex CO5 7DR
(01206) 729414
Exotic plants, including orchids

Frontiers
37–39 Pembridge Road
Notting Hill
London W11 3HG
(020) 7727 6132

Glenhirst Cactus Nursery
Station Road
Swineshead
Nr. Boston
Lincolnshire PE20 3NX
(01205) 820314
www.glenhirstcact:andpalms.co.uk
Cacti and other desert plants

Grimsdyke House
12 Southcourt Avenue
Bexhill-on-Sea
East Sussex TN39 3AR
(01424) 221452
Bougainvillea

Heal and Son
Tottenham Court Road
London W1T 7LQ
(020) 7636 1666
www.heals.co.uk
Range of pots and containers

Ikea
branches throughout the UK
www.ikea.com

J & D Marston
Culag
Green Lane
Nafferton
Driffield
East Yorkshire YO25 0LF
(01377) 254487
Ferns

Jekka's Herb Farm
Rose Cottage
Shellards Lane
Alveston
Bristol
Avon BS35 3SY
(01454) 418878
www.jekkasherb.demon.co.uk

Kara Kara
2a Pond Place
London SW3 6QJ
(020) 7591 0891
Japanese handmade ceramics, etc.

Keith Brymer Jones
Highgate Pottery
199 Archway Road
London N6 5BN
(020) 8347 8186
Handmade porcelain and stoneware pots

McBeans Orchids
Cooksbridge
Lewes
Sussex BN8 4PR
(01273) 400228

Muji
41 Carnaby Street
London W1V 1PD
(020) 7221 9360
Modern Japanese ware

Mulu Nurseries
Burford House
Tenbury Wells
Worcestershire WR15 8HQ
(01584) 811592
www.mulu.co.uk
Exotic plants

New Covent Garden Market
(wholesale market for plants and flowers)
London SW8 5NX

Newington Nurseries
Newington
Wallingford
Oxfordshire OX10 7AW
(01865) 400533
Conservatory plants and herbs

Nimmo and Spooner
277 Lillie Road
London SW6 7LL
(020) 7385 2724
Antique French and Mediterranean
pots and ceramics

Nom
150 Walton Street
London SW3 2JJ
(020) 7584 4158
Vietnamese lacquer ware

Reads Nursery
Hales Hall
Loddon
Norfolk NR14 6QW
(01508) 548395
www.readsnursery.co.uk
Conservatory plants, including
Citrus

Selfridges
400 Oxford Street
London W1
(020) 7629 1234
www.selfridges.com
Range of pots and containers

Stonehurst Nurseries
Selsfield Road
Ardingly
Haywards Heath
Sussex RH17 6TN
(01444) 892488
www.stonehurstnurseries.com
Orchids

The Chelsea Gardener
125 Sydney Street
London SW3 6NR
(020) 7352 5656

The Conran Shop
Michelin House
81 Fulham Road
London SW3 6RD
(020) 7589 7401
www.conran.com
Range of pots and containers

The Conservatory
Gomshall Gallery
Gomshall
Surrey GU5 9LB
(01483) 203019
www.conservatoryplants.com
Conservatory and house plants

The Ivory Tower
464 Muswell Hill Broadway
London N10 1BS
(020) 8444 1070
Unusual containers

The Old Walled Garden
Oxonhoath
Hadlow
Kent TN11 9SS
(01732) 810012
Conservatory plants, especially Australian

The Palm Centre
Ham Central Nursery
Ham Street
Ham
Richmond
Surrey TW10 7HA
(020) 8255 6191
www.palmcentre.co.uk
Palms, cycads, and other exotics

The Palm Farm
Thornton Hall Gardens
Station Road
Thornton Curtis
Nr. Ulceby
Humberside DN39 6XF
(01469) 531232
Conservatory plants

The Photosynthesist
2a Bathwick Villas
Henrietta Road
Bath
Avon BA2 6LS
Contemporary planters

Toobees Exotics
(Office) 20 Inglewood
St Johns
Woking
Surrey GU21 3HX
(01483) 797534
www.cactus-mall.com/toobees
Wide range of exotics

Trebah Enterprises Ltd
Trebah
Mawnan Smith
Falmouth
Cornwall TR11 5JZ
(01326) 250448
www.trebah-garden.co.uk
Agave and conservatory climbers

Uzumara Orchids
9 Port Henderson
Gairloch
Rosshire
Scotland IV21 2AS
(01445) 741228
http://freespace.virgin.net/i.la_croix
African and Madagascan orchids

Westdale Nurseries
Holt Road
Bradford-on-Avon
Wiltshire BA15 1TS
(01225) 863258
Bougainvillea

Whichford Pottery
Whichford
Shipston-on-Stour
Warwickshire CV36 5PG
(01608) 684416
www.whichfordpottery.com
Hand-thrown terracotta pots
and containers

GENERAL **INDEX**

ACKNOWLEDGMENTS

Author's Acknowledgments

I would like to thank the following for their help in creating *Hip Houseplants*: Vickie for her constant support; Jennifer d'Abo and the crew at Moyses Stevens for opening my eyes and allowing me to learn and develop; my assistant "Little Gem" thanks for being a "second pair of eyes" and for all those late nights; Jeremy Hopley, with assistants Liberty Silver and Rachel Warne, for the brilliant photography and supply of top-class CDs; Wei Tang for her innate sense of style; Doctor Frisbee and Doctor Thomas Johansen for the loan of their home.

The team from Dorling Kindersley: the dynamic duo, Judith More and Janis Utton, for their invaluable contribution; Neil Lockley for his patience and encouragement; Wendy Bartlet for all her hard work.

Also thanks to all at Arnott and Mason for their help with plants and verification; Craig of Quality Plants; Steve and Adam at H. Miles; C. Best for all the containers; the splendid Rob Cassy for all his advice.

Thank you to the following for the loan of various items: Aria for the black ceramic vases and fake fur throw on pages 24–25; ASA for containers on pages 10–11; Capital Garden Centre for the containers on pages 20–21 and the terracotta and stone pots on pages 22–23; Carden Cunietti for the cushions, throw, lampshade, stand, and set of boxes on pages 16–17, cushion, lampshade, stand, and small pony skin boxes on pages 24–25; Ceramica Blue for the large black tiles on pages 24–25; The Ivory Tower for the containers on pages 18–19, the large wooden urn containers and striped box on pages 24–25, and all items on pages 26–27; Kara Kara for the table on pages 16–17; Keith Brymer Jones for containers on pages 10–11 and for pages 28–29; Muji for the sofa on pages 16–17; Nimmo and Spooner for the large antique pots on pages 22–23; Nom for the tray, pot, large bamboo platter, and bowl on pages 16–17.

Publisher's Acknowledgments

Dorling Kindersley would like to thank Ann Parry for compiling the index.